Communicating in the Workplace ▲

SUSAN K. OLSON, Ph.D.
PAUL M. OLSON, M.A.

ALORAY INC.
PROFESSIONAL & ACADEMIC PUBLISHER

Library of Congress Cataloging-in-Publication Data

Olson, Susan K., 1954-
    Communicating in the workplace / Susan K. Olson, Paul M. Olson.
       p.   cm.
    Includes bibliographical references and index.
    ISBN 0-913690-16-3 : $29.95 (est.)
    1. Communication in personnel management. 2. Communication in
organizations.   I. Olson, Paul M., 1958- .   II. Title.
HF5549.5.C6045   1992
650.1'3--dc20

                                              92-27889
                                                  CIP

TABLE OF CONTENTS

Preface   v

1. **Introduction**   **1**
   Communication and Success   6
   Communication Problems in Business   7
   The Illusion of Communication   8
   The Competent Communicator   9
   Communication Attitudes   10
   Communication Styles   15
   Communication Games   22
   Healthy Communication   24

2. **The Communication Process**   **27**
   A Model of Communication   27
   The Process of Organizing and Communication   29
   Organizational Communication   31
   Key Steps for Improving Organizational Communication   33
   The Importance of Climate   36
   Prescription for a Healthy Climate   37
   Summary   39

3. **Motivating through Communication**   **41**
   Communication as a Management Tool   41
   Using Communication Techniques to Improve Performance   43
   Active Listening   44
   Feedback   52
   Managers' Expectations: The Self-Fulfilling Prophecy   54
   Employee Needs   57
   Giving Clear Instructions   58
   How Can You Put Communication to Work?   59

4. **Interpersonal Influence**   **61**
   Interpersonal Influence and Trust   61
   Dimensions of a Trusting Relationship   63
   Power in Relationships   65
   Calibrated Disclosure   65
   Other Motivating Techniques   73
   Motivation: A Value-for-Value Exchange   75
   Motivating through Positive Reinforcement   76

5. **One-to-One Communication**   **81**
   The Importance of One-to-One Communication   81
   Planning for One-to-One Communication   82
   Conducting the Exchange   87

6. **Employment and Appraisal Interviewing   89**
   The Employment Interview   89
   Performance Appraisal Interviews   105

7. **Conflict   113**
   Organizational Rewards   113
   Conflict in Change: A Necessary Condition   114
   Elements of Conflict   114
   Conflict Structure   117
   Characteristics of Conflict   118
   Cooperation versus Competition   120

8. **Managing Conflict   123**
   Conflict Management Styles   123
   Relational Styles   125
   Increasing Your Power   125
   Managing Conflict for Productivity   126
   Effective Conflict Skills   133
   Your Own Conflicts   134
   A Checklist for Managers   135

9. **Conducting Effective Meetings   137**
   Problems with Meetings   137
   Is a Meeting Necessary?   138
   The Need for an Agenda   139
   Conducting the Meeting   140
   Creating a Positive Climate   142
   Productive Problem Solving   143
   Ending the Meeting   144
   Follow-up Measures   145
   Getting More Out of Meetings You Attend   146

10. **Management Presentations that Make a Difference   153**
   Your Stake in Presentations   153
   The Competent Speaker   154
   Presenting Yourself   155
   The Three-Step Process   156
   Question-and-Answer Sessions   177
   Audience Turnoffs   178
   Room Setup   179

References   181

Index   185

PREFACE

Just like time, we cannot reverse our communication. This cannot be emphasized enough. As professor, author, consultant, corporate director, manager, or scholar, we have taught, lectured, facilitated, researched, and practiced the art of communicating. Each time a session begins, two fundamental laws are made very explicit: (1) communication is irreversible (once we say something it cannot be taken back) and (2) all communication is persuasive (every time we communicate—or choose not to—we impact others whether we intend to or not). Without a doubt these laws will be predominant throughout our professional life.

The most effective communicator can be identified by and understands that influence is something others experience when in his or her presence. It is the way we treat people that makes one influential, and the way we do it is by communicating. The most skilled communicators use their influence to empower others. This is a perspective that is finally beginning to appear in the management literature that has long been awaited.

Unfortunately, those who communicate poorly cannot reverse the gross effects their mistakes create for others, literally leaving emotional scars on their receivers, whether they be employees, customers or, worse yet, children.

On the average, a small 4 percent of the people in this country are clear, direct, effective communicators, leaving a majority of 96 percent who could use fine tuning if not major repairs. One of the top-ranked fears of nearly 50 percent of Americans is the fear of presenting oneself before others. Looking at these statistics, we question why communication is not a required subject matter at any educational level.

It is rare that we receive proper training in good communication skills. Communication skill is not innate; rather, it is learned. Although we communicate daily, our communication skills need to be practiced and refined, while poor communication habits can be unlearned, which is the reason for writing this book.

Our research on effective communication and managerial success clearly shows that lack of communication skills is a major problem in business today. In fact, many managers have been trained to do the opposite of what this book advocates. Business and management literature is abundant with surveys to support the claim that communication is the weakest skill area for managers, the skill most business schools fail to address, leaving many managers unprepared for the job of managing people.

This book is not a cure for poor communication practices; rather, it is a prescription for healthy communication skills. Practical application is what makes a difference. Whether it is interpersonal communication, business communication, or public communication, the fundamental laws still apply. This book focuses on effective communication skills at each level—one to one, groups and meetings, interviews, giving management presentations, managing people, and dealing with conflict.

Who is this book for? For those who manage or deal with people—in other words—everyone.

Susan Olson, Ph.D.

Paul Olson, M.A.

1
Introduction ▲

Just as we learned the skill of walking, running, or playing a game, we learned rudimentary skills of listening, talking, and responding as we grew and developed from infancy through adulthood. Most people go through life with the skills they acquired without being fully aware of their degree of effectiveness. Few go on to practice and perfect their skills to be as effective and influential as possible.

If you were going to run a marathon, you would not simply rely on the running skills you gained in childhood and hope to win the race. Most runners would spend months in rigorous practice. The same applies to communicating. To effectively communicate, we need to perfect and polish our skills for the ultimate advantage: influencing other people. Communication is indeed both a practiced art and a rigorous science.

The ability to communicate effectively is not gained easily. To be an effective communicator requires constant training. This chapter will introduce you to the basics of communication; bring to light some facts about communicating; reveal the importance of communication, particularly in business; and explore typical problems and solutions for any member of an organization.

To start with, here are some thoughts about communication:

When you communicate, you teach others how to treat you.

This is known as the Theory of Reciprocity or the Golden Rule. The way we communicate shows others the way we would like them to treat us. In essence, you need to give to others what you want to get.

For example, the first time you meet someone you have a choice in how you greet that person. You can either be warm and friendly or cold and hostile. If you choose to be warm and friendly, you are likely to receive a warm and friendly response. If you choose to be cold, aloof, or hostile, you teach the other to respond to you in the same fashion. This is called the mirror response. You receive what you give to others. The mirror response is your communication reflected back to you.

In addition, the way you behave toward another adjusts to meet the roles you play in society. Some specific roles, such as manager, supervisor, staff advisor, parent, or teacher, naturally place you in a dominant role, while roles such as subordinate or junior member of a committee place you in a submissive role. As a coworker, your role is likely equal to that of another. Yet if you act dominant, you can almost guarantee your coworker will respond to you submissively.

Generally, then, others will complement your role behavior. If you use dominant communication behavior, you will elicit submissive behavior in others. If you are submissive in your communication behavior, you will elicit the opposite response (dominance) in others.

While your attitude of warmth or hostility is mirrored back to you, your role behavior will tell the other how to react, either with dominance or submissiveness. Figure 1.1 demonstrates how role behavior and attitudes interact.

Figure 1.1   Interaction of Role Behavior and Attitudes

Source: Timothy Leary, *Interpersonal Diagnosis of Personality* (New York, Ronald, 1957).

People respond to you as they do because you teach them how to treat you through attitude and action. With practice, you can manage your behavior so that others perceive and respond to you in a desired and predictable fashion. In doing so, you can largely determine the outcome of your communication with others.

When communicating, you influence others whether you intend to or not.

We are always communicating. In fact, we cannot not communicate. *How* we communicate is more important than the actual words we use. Even choosing not to communicate gives a message to others. You may be familiar with the experience of waiting at the boss's desk while he occupies himself with paperwork, communicating to you that he is busy and you'll just have to wait. By waiting in silence for a while, you indicate that although no words were spoken, you understand the message.

You also communicate much more than you intend to communicate. When we communicate we express ourselves with body language and facial expression (55 percent), vocal inflections (35 percent), and only 7 percent with the words we use (Mehrabian and Weiner, 1967, pp. 109–114). Furthermore, if your words conflict with your facial expression and body language, others will believe your nonverbal message rather than the spoken one. A simple "no" may mean "yes" or "maybe" depending on how it is said and the context of the communication. This context includes not only the present space and time dimensions but often past history.

Your communication is persuasive.

Everything we say and do influences others. Problems arise in communication when we fail to acknowledge that we have an effect on others. The words we use, how we use them, our body language during communication, and even silence contribute toward changing behavior in others. Every facet of communication has an influence upon others. Becoming aware of how communication affects others gives you more control over the effects of your communication.

To assess how aware you are of the impact of your communication on others, ask yourself the following questions:

1. Is your communication positive?
2. Does your communication help others to feel good about themselves?
3. Do others enjoy communicating with you and seek you out when they need to talk?
4. Can others be open, honest, and direct with you?

OR

1. Are you generally negative in your communication with others?
2. Do you manipulate and play games to get your way?
3. Are others afraid to tell you the truth?
4. Do you feel out of control in your communication with others?

You have a choice. If you don't exercise your communication options, you give up control over events and circumstances that surround you. Since you have a choice, you need to be image conscious and make sure your communication is positive. Being aware of how you communicate enables you to use communication to your advantage.

When you communicate, you usually operate on the basis of perceptions and feelings more than facts.

No two people are likely to perceive an event in exactly the same manner. We each have different backgrounds, past experiences, social roles, and personalities, and therefore view the world differently. For example, when a safety manager looks at a new piece of equipment, he sees its accident potential and possible dollar losses. The engineer who designed it, however, looks at the hidden maintenance costs stemming from preproduction decisions.

The perceptions we hold about people, words, and events have a tremendous impact upon our communication, our behavior, and our expectations. It is perception that causes the various interpretations, and the potential consequences of such variance can be tremendous. Consider the following examples:

- A manager may observe a shortage in the cash register one morning and suspect that one of five employees may be absconding with store profits. The next day the manager sees one salesperson open the register with a "no sale" transaction. The manager acts on his perception that the employee is taking cash. Not having access to the facts behind the situation, the manager reprimands the employee for doing so. The employee, having been told by the assistant manager to open the register to obtain petty cash to purchase something, is completely offended by the actions of the manager.

- A manager has been told that an employee has been arriving late to work for the past few days. The manager casually watches the time while walking by the employee's work station. The employee perceives the manager checking the clock each morning when he arrives and based on that perception feels as though the manager does not trust him. Regardless of the real reason for his tardiness, the manager will act on his perception and the employee on his.

A good rule of thumb to follow is "When in doubt, check it out." Had the first manager asked the employee if he or she was told to take cash from the register, much misunderstanding would have been prevented. Had the second manager asked the employee about his tardiness, feelings of resentment might have been prevented and the relationship maintained.

The role of perception is easily seen in the employment interview. An interviewer forms an impression of the applicant within the first four minutes of the interview and spends the rest of the interview looking for information to support that perception. When the interview is not well structured, interviewers make a decision based solely on perceptions, regardless of the applicant's qualifications.

While it may be argued that the first information people receive about you is relatively unimportant, perceptions and first impressions are valid for the perceiver and can be lasting. Changing first perceptions takes a great deal of effort. Communicate what you want others to know about you to prevent unfavorable perceptions. We all have the ability to manage our impression to our advantage and to improve our communication with others.

When you communicate, you reveal and exchange values.

The content and form of your communication reveal your value structure and that of your organization or department. You communicate the relative worth you attribute to things, people, and events in your life. You reveal to others what you desire and to what degree the object of your desire is important to you. Conversely, much of the time we may hold certain values but not say or do things that reflect these values. For effective communication, it is important to strive for consistency between what you value and believe and what you say and do.

Consider the store with Customer Is King printed on its bags in which the salespeople nevertheless treat customers as though they are a nuisance. Look at your behavior and check to see if what you say follows what you know your values to be. Check out this understanding with others to see if they agree with your own evaluation of the balance you have among your values, what you say, and how you behave.

When you communicate, you are responsible for your expectations.

Each time we communicate we expect something. Expectations we have for communication events vary, depending upon the situation and the people involved. Most of us expect a certain reward for the effort expended in communicating with others. Whether it is economic status, social belonging, personal benefits, or self-esteem, a reward is expected. If rewards are not forthcoming, we will change our expectations (what is wanted from the communication), behavior (what is brought to the exchange), and attitude (how we feel about the other or the relationship itself).

When our expectations are not met we tend to blame others, the situation, or other circumstances. When disappointments, problems, and frustrations arise in communication, they usually stem from unstated expectations. We frequently give clues as to what we expect. Achieving expectations requires that we become aware of the potential inaccuracies that may exist. We need to make our expectations clear, to make implicit expectations explicit.

When expectations are met, the feelings experienced are satisfaction, a positive sense of self-esteem, greater control, and a more realistic sense for future expectations. Success in communication demands establishing realistic expectations and taking responsibility for meeting them.

When you communicate, you do more than communicate information; you also comment on your relationship.

Each time you speak you not only offer information but you also make a statement about your relationship with the person you are speaking to. You convey information about your power and status, degree of intimacy, and attraction simply through your tone of voice, choice of words, and body language. Often we are not aware of our relational communication.

Figure 1.2   Effects of Communication

When you communicate:

- You teach others how to treat you.
- You influence others whether you intend to or not.
- Your communication is persuasive.
- You usually operate on the basis of perceptions and feelings more than facts.
- You reveal and exchange values.
- You are responsible for your expectations.
- You do more than communicate information; you also comment on your relationship.

COMMUNICATION AND SUCCESS

Recent research indicates that communication skills are the most important skills in determining managerial success, above accounting, financial, or computer skills. In a study conducted at the University of Minnesota (see Table 1.1), business administration alumni were asked to rank order skills most important for managerial success. Communication (oral and written) was at the top of their list (Foster et al., 1978). Even engineers recognize the importance of communication skills in business. Graduates from Colorado State University's Engineering College rated courses in communication as more important than their senior engineering design course ("Instruction in Communication," unpublished survey, 1979).

Subscribers to the *Harvard Business Review* rated the ability to communicate as the most important characteristic of a promotable executive, rating communication higher than ambition, education, and capacity for hard work (Bowman, 1964).

When 170 well-known business and industrial firms were asked to list the most common reasons for not offering jobs to applicants, the most frequent replies were "inability to communicate" and "poor communication skills" (Endicott, 1979).

Table 1.1   Importance of Skills
University of Minnesota Study

	Percent responding "Very Important"	
	Bachelor's Degree	MBA Degree
Oral Communication	92	95
Written Communication	86	94
Decision Making and Problem Solving	82	86
Time Management	60	56
Interpersonal Skills	44	66
Business Strategy	44	56
Interviewing and Resume Preparation	31	19
Assertiveness and Sensitivity Training	45	32
Computer Usage	35	27
Small-Group or Team Processes	36	44
Organizational Politics	27	35

Source: Foster et al. "A Market Study for the College of Business Administration," unpublished survey, University of Minnesota, Twin Cities, Minneapolis, 1978).

Communication skill has long been recognized as representative of leadership and human competence. The desire to communicate and the artistry displayed by employees' communication represent a significant portion of a manager's perception of eEmployees. Simply put, the more one skillfully interacts with others about organizational goals and procedures, the more one is likely to be regarded as a leader and as competent.

COMMUNICATION PROBLEMS IN BUSINESS

One survey of nearly one hundred companies indicated that managers spend 75 to 80 percent of their time communicating, yet in over seven surveys communication is consistently listed as their major weakness. The authors of the best-selling *In Search of Excellence* (Peters and Waterman, 1982) argue that today's executives and management students have been miseducated and that managers are out of touch with their people. The two major weaknesses in today's managers are the lack of communication skills and the inability to deal with uncertainty.

In a symposium at Case Western Reserve University, management theorists shared their ideas about successful managers. They agreed that the ability to communicate is indispensable to management, yet skill in communcation is one that few management programs teach (Srivastva, 1983). Having surveyed business schools and their curriculum, we found that few, if any, offer a course in communication, leaving prospective managers relatively unprepared for the job of managing. Peters and Waterman go even further, saying that if schools do offer such a course, it is usually centered around rational problem solving and uses case studies rather than practical experience, thus training managers to be technocrats who later wonder why they are not liked or respected. It is our opinion that the study of managing needs to go beyond classical managerial functions of planning, organizing, directing, and controlling to include influence and persuasion through communication.

THE ILLUSION OF COMMUNICATION

We often assume communication has taken place when it really hasn't. We tend to think that saying something to our satisfaction will result in effective communication. For example, the manager who announced a new policy at the staff meeting might assume his message was sufficient; however, if he had backed it up with a written memorandum and system changes, he could better ensure that his message would be received by all employees.

It is easy to simply get something off your chest and express it to someone else. It is not quite as easy to make sure you are completely understood. Effective communication requires that we use a variety of tools to get our message across and ensure understanding.

Feedback from others is a tool we can use to determine whether our message is clearly understood. This requires that we focus on the receiver for accurate understanding rather than on the relief we feel by simply expressing ourselves. There are many tools to use and methods for promoting effective communication that will be explored in this chapter.

We may think we're communicating when we are not. A number of assumptions can hinder real communication, such as those that follow.

We assume the word itself has meaning.

The meaning of a word depends upon the context in which it is used. Take, for example, a boss saying to a subordinate, "I'd like to see you in my office." The meaning of this set of words for the subordinate may be, "I did something wrong," while the meaning for the boss may be, "He's going to get a promotion." The context, the setting, the way the words are uttered, and the nonverbal behaviors that accompany the words are what determine the real meaning of the statement.

We assume our message can only be expressed in one way.

There are a number of different ways to express a message. If you want to wrap up a work group meeting so that your employees can get back to work, there are a number of ways to do so, and each will have a different impact on the employees: "We've wasted too much time here; you need to get back to work." "This was a productive meeting, and I'm looking forward to our next one." "I'm out of time; we'll have to meet again next week for the rest of the agenda items." Consider your goal or purpose before uttering your message. This will help you to more effectively express yourself for the desired effect.

We assume people are perfect communicators.

Problems arise because people are imperfect communicators. We need to learn to accept this fact and adapt to our given situation, realizing that we may have to go one step further to improve our communication with others. We can't prevent all problems from occurring, but we can learn to adapt to situations.

THE COMPETENT COMMUNICATOR

It is easy to characterize an effective communicator and less easy to find one. The effective communicator has an impact on others. The effective communicator helps others to feel good about themselves, while expressing his or her ideas clearly. To do this, the effective communicator focuses on the receiver of the message rather than on the message alone. The effective communicator is sensitive to each communication situation and the people involved. He can adapt his words and behavior to meet the needs of each situation, no matter how different the circumstances may be. In other words, the effective communicator is flexible rather than rigid in his attempts to communicate with others.

Ineffective communicators say what they have to say regardless of the situation or else communicate only the information others want to hear. In some organizations such communication behavior is rewarded, which would explain why communication is a major problem in business. The key is balance between these two extremes. The effective communicator also takes ownership for his thoughts and feelings rather than giving others power to make him feel or act a certain way. In this same vein, the effective communicator takes responsibility for and defines his or her expectations, rather than waiting for someone else to meet those expectations or blaming others for not meeting them.

In total, an effective communicator uses the skills described in detail in this book. These skills include focusing on the receiver, establishing trust, soliciting and adapting to feedback, achieving empathy, using calibrated disclosure, and using appropriate listening and responding skills. Because of his skill in these areas, the effective communicator commands a great deal of interpersonal power among those he encounters.

Effective Communication Skills on the Job

The effective communicator exhibits the following behaviors:

- Gives advice without ordering or directing
- Corrects erroneous behavior without upsetting the other
- Uses performance evaluations to motivate improved performance
- Gives rewards connected with and immediately following performance
- Gives clear instructions
- Anticipates mistakes before they happen
- Referees conflict without angering either party
- Stimulates people to meet emergency situations
- Persuades others to do more than they believed they could
- Engages in friendly persuasion without destroying the opposition
- Tolerates differences and respects opinions of others
- Maintains equality in the distribution of rewards and punishments
- Avoids gossip and rumors
- Provides accurate, complete information
- Gives reasons for decisions
- Spots and develops potential in subordinates
- Knows how to ask questions and whom to ask
- Encourages others to take the lead

Skillful management of communication enables you to achieve your goals. In other words, you can maintain positive control though communication.

COMMUNICATION ATTITUDES

In order to more fully understand communication, let's explore some common attitudes people have about communicating. Our attitude toward communicating will probably change with regard to the situation in which we are involved. However, there are three common attitudes frequently found in business today. To understand these three attitudes, refer to Figure 1.3.

Figure 1.3   Attitude Scale

Demanding   Sensitive   Pleasing

The first attitude is Demanding. As the name implies, this person says whatever he or she has to say regardless of the situation. This attitude is not one of compromise. This attitude considers the self as most important. The person holding such an attitude would never even consider changing his or her words appropriately to fit the situation.

The second attitude is one on the opposite side of the spectrum. The Pleasing attitude adapts too easily to the situation. If you were to ask a Pleaser what he or she would like to do, the typical response would be, "I don't care; whatever you want is fine with me." While it may sound as if the Pleaser is being courteous, if such responses are repeated over time, the Pleaser never gets any needs met.

The third attitude is in the center of the spectrum. It is the Sensitive attitude. The sensitive person takes a look at the immediate situation and the people involved and then decides on the most appropriate way to phrase his or her communication. The Sensitive person understands that to be effective in communication, one must be willing to adapt to the needs of the situation. In other words, the Sensitive person recognizes that there are a number of ways to express an idea and chooses the best method for the audience and occasion.

While there are times when a Demanding attitude is useful, there are times when it is not so effective. Let's say that you need to confront a subordinate about unsafe behavior. More than likely the Demanding attitude would work well because the situation requires you be straightforward and direct. However, using this attitude in every situation would not promote effective communication.

In addition, the Pleasing attitude would be effective in dealing with an employee with personal problems. In this situation, you would not want to be direct but concerned for what the other wants to say.

The key to the Sensitive attitude is that the person using it has the ability to assess the situation and adapt his or her communication accordingly. It may require that the Sensitive person change to the Pleasing or Demanding attitude. Sensitive people often say, "It depends on the situation."

Take a few moments and complete the inventory in Figure 1.4. This inventory will indicate which attitude you typically use in your communication behavior.

Figure 1.4   RHETSEN Scale

Instructions: Listed below are a number of statements to which you are to indicate your degree of agreement. Please consider each statement individually and check the column that best represents how true each is. You are marking your attitudes. There are no right or wrong answers.

Column A: almost always true
Column B: frequently true
Column C: sometimes true
Column D: infrequently true
Column E: almost never true

How true is each statement?

	A	B	C	D	E
1. People should be frank and spontaneous in conversation.					
2. An idea can be communicated in many different ways.					
3. When talking with someone with swhom you disagree, you should feel obligated to state your opinion.					
4. A person should laugh at an unfunny joke just to please the joke-teller.					
5. It's good to follow the rule: before blowing your top at someone, sleep on the problem.					
6. When talking to others, you should drop all your defenses.					
7. It is best to hide one's true feelings in order to avoid hurting others.					
8. No matter how hard you try, you just can't make friends with everyone.					
9. One should keep quiet rather than say something which will alienate others.					
10. You should share your joys with your closest friends.					
11. It is acceptable to discuss religion with a stranger.					
12. A supervisor in a work situation must be forceful with subordinates to be effective.					
13. A person should tell it like it is.					
14. "Look before you leap" is the most important rule to follow when talking to others.					
15. You should tell friends if you think they are making a mistake.					
16. The first thing that comes to mind is the best thing to say.					
17. When conversing, you should tell others what they want to hear.					

How true is each statement?

	A	B	C	D	E

18. When someone dominates the conversation, it's important to interrupt them in order to state your opinion.

19. When angry, a person should say nothing rather than say something he or she will be sorry for later.

20. When someone has an irritating habit, he or she should be told about it.

21. When talking to your friends, you should adjust your remarks to suit them.

22. You really can't put sugar coating on bad news.

23. A person who speaks his or her gut feeling, is to be admired.

24. You shouldn't make a scene in a restaurant by arguing with a waiter.

25. Putting thoughts into words just the way you want them is a difficult process.

26. A friend who has bad breath should be told about it.

27. If you're sure you're right, you should argue with a person who disagrees with you.

28. If people would open up to each other the world would be better off.

29. There is a difference between someone who is "diplomatic" and one who is "two-faced."

30. You should tell people if you think they are about to embarrass themselves.

31. One should not be afraid to voice his or her opinion.

32. If your boss doesn't like you, there's not much you can do about it.

33. You should tell someone if you think they are giving you bad advice.

34. Saying what you think is a sign of friendship.

35. When you're sure you're right, you should press your point until you win the argument.

36. "If you feel it, say it" is a good rule to follow in conversation.

37. If a man cheats on his wife, he should tell her.

38. It is better to speak your gut feelings than to beat around the bush.

39. We should have a kind word for the people we meet in life.

40. One should treat all people in the same way.

RHETSEN Score Sheet

Instructions: Circle the number in each column that corresponds to your attitude checked for each item. Repeat for each of the three scales.

	S Scale					D Scale					P Scale				
	A	B	C	D	E	A	B	C	D	E	A	B	C	D	E
1.		1	2	1		2	1							1	2
2.															
3.		1	2	1		2	1							1	2
4.		1	2	1					1	2	2	1			
5.		1	2	1					1	2	2	1			
6.															
7.		1	2	1					1	2	2	1			
8.															
9.		1	2	1					1	2	2	1			
10.															
11.		1	2	1		2	1								
12.														1	2
13.		1	2	1		2	1							1	2
14.															
15.		1	2	1		2	1							1	2
16.		1	2	1		2	1							1	2
17.		1	2	1					1	2	2	1			
18.		1	2	1		2	1							1	2
19.		1	2	1							2	1			
20.		1	2	1		2	1							1	2
21.		1	2	1					1	2					
22.															
23.		1	2	1		2	1							1	2
24.		1	2	1							2	1			
25.															
26.		1	2	1		2	1							1	2
27.		1	2	1		2	1							1	2
28.		1	2	1		2	1							1	2
29.															
30.		1	2	1		2	1							1	2
31.		1	2	1		2	1								
32.															
33.		1	2	1		2	1							1	2
34.		1	2	1		2	1							1	2
35.		1	2	1		2	1							1	2
36.															
37.		1	2	1											
38.		1	2	1		2	1							1	2
39.		1	2	1											
40.															
Totals	__	__	__	__	__	__	__	__	__	__	__	__	__	__	__

Source: Roderick P. Hart, Robert E. Carlson, and William F. Eadie, "Attitudes toward Communication and the Assessment of Rhetorical Sensitivity," *Communication Monographs*, Vol. 47 (Annandale, VA: Speech Communication Association, March 1980).

Interpreting your results:

Demanding:	Pleasing:	Sensitive:
Low 0 – 9	Low 0 – 7	Low 24 and below
Average 10 – 20	Average 8 – 10	Average 25 – 37
High 21 and above	High 10 and above	High 38 and above

In a 1985 study that included five different industries, the authors found that a majority of managers have the demanding attitude. This may explain why communication is so often mentioned as a weakness in management. Ideally, we would hope that the most successful managers are sensitive, allowing them to be better communicators and more influential leaders (Olson, 1985).

COMMUNICATION STYLES

There are five basic styles of communication. Much of the time we communicate with mixed styles and mixed intentions. Understanding each style will help to develop an appreciation for the appropriate and inappropriate uses of each. A person with only a limited repertoire of communication styles has a difficult time expressing him or herself effectively with others. Understanding each style makes it easier to adapt your message so that you are better understood by people who use styles other than that which you use. As you will see, each style develops from the three communication attitudes.

In each communication event, we have a choice as to how much we consider the person we are talking to. Simultaneously, we have a choice as to how involved we get personally or, in other words, how much we are willing to disclose to others.

The styles can be plotted on a matrix, as shown in Figure 1.5, with the variables (1) attention to others and (2) personal involvement.

Figure 1.5   Communication Styles

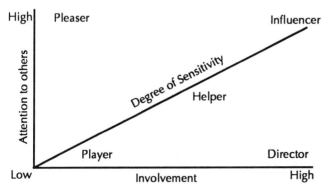

The Player

The Player's communication is playful and friendly. It is characterized by the following kinds of messages:

Small talk: "How do you like this weather we've been having?"
Observations and descriptions: "I notice you got a new car."
Reporting events: "We went to the game last night. The Lakers won."
Factual information: "Twelve people have signed up to go."
Story-telling: "Did you hear the one about . . ."
Personal preferences: "I'd prefer the green over the blue."
Feelings: "I'm tired and hungry," or "This room seems cold to me."

The Player's communication is also characterized by personal pronouns such as I, me, my, and mine. When you want to pass time with another, distance yourself, or keep things moving, the Player's communication works well (Nunally, Miller, and Wackman, 1975).

Usually during the Player's growth and development, he or she has learned to use this style either because it worked or because he or she has not developed a strong sense of self-esteem. With a low sense of self-worth, we typically do not reveal very much to others, and as a result, others don't have the opportunity to get to know us. If this style is used and works well, there is a tendency to continue the style even when the situation suggests that it is not appropriate.

Typically, the Player grows up in an environment where the message "Children should be seen and not heard" is prevalent. The Player learns that what he or she has to say is not important and that it is not okay to disclose one's feelings. The Player operates with this style because he or she needs to get the immediate attention of others to feel accepted socially and to feel alright about himself or herself. Usually after a quick exchange of small talk, the player feels uncomfortable in engaging in any kind of dialogue. As one research group puts it, "You really don't have to have much skill when you're using this style because it has low involvement and concern for others. These statements disclose little about yourself. If you were to discuss important issues using this style you'll probably sound detached and disconnected from what's happening" (Nunally, Miller, and Wackman, 1975, pp. 173–79).

The Director

The Director usually wants to force change in another person or situation—with a particular goal in mind. The Director makes many interpretations (who or what's wrong or right) and seeks control (what you should or should not do). We usually use this style when we want to be persuasive or to try to control what is happening or when it will happen. The Director operates from a very demanding attitude. In everyday conversations this style is very common. Most selling, bargaining, promoting, advocating, preaching, and lecturing reflect the Director's style.

The Director's style of communication can be characterized by the following:

Directing: "We've got to increase sales by at least 10%!"
Giving solutions: "Here's what you should do."
Persuading: "Come on, let's try it just once."
Evaluating: "You're wrong again."
Blaming, criticizing: "You're never on time."
Ventilation: "Who's he to tell me what to do?"
Complaining: "I do all the dirty work around here and never get any help."
Self-protecting: "That's not what I said," or "I didn't mean that."
(Nunally, Miller, and Wackman, 1975)

The Director style includes speaking for others, closed questions, "why" questions, demands, blame or challenges, and imperatives. Key words include should, ought, have to, need to, always, never, every, right and wrong, or good and bad.

As Nuunally and associates point out, "Trying to change or control an outcome can stifle creativity and vitality in a relationship. Most people resist change because the underlying message is 'You're wrong' or 'I don't need to change, you do.' With resistance comes the temptation to increase the pressure. If you try to apply more pressure to force change, this style can easily backfire. The result can be misunderstanding and hurt feelings. (Nunally, Miller, and Wackman, 1975, pp. 180–85).

The Director most likely grew up in an environment in which he or she received little direction and little positive feedback, resulting in the Director having to prove his or her worth. This style allows the Director to sense the control and esteem he or she seeks. The Director has a strong need for control.

The Helper

Rather than trying to keep things smooth or trying to control, the Helper's goal is to foster nurturance. By helping others, the Helper feels needed, thereby increasing his or her sense of self-esteem.

Typical helping behaviors include the following:

Offering answers: "No, this is how it works."
    Offering assistance: "Let me help you with that."
Speculating: "Do you think you're tired today because of our meeting yesterday?"
Searching for reasons: "I wonder if it's because you've been working late recently."
Posing solutions: "Maybe we could develop a budget to control our spending together."
Encouraging others: "You're doing a great job, keep it up."
(Nunally, Miller, and Wackman, 1975)

The Helper makes a limited use of disclosure skills. The intention is to assist and nurture others so that others will turn to the Helper in times of need. The Helper has a moderate degree of self-esteem. The level of self-esteem rises when positive feedback is received from those helped. In situations where help is not required, the Helper experiences a lowered level of self-esteem. The Helper needs others to feel okay about himself or herself.

It is likely that the Helper learned deference over assertiveness as a child. In other words, the child was taught to defer to what others wanted rather than to think about and decide what he or she really wanted. This style of communication is appropriate in some situations, but it can be considered a form of manipulation as well. While the intentions sound kind and friendly, the degree of concern for others must be checked. The Helper style used excessively can backfire into martyrdom. Characteristic language includes the use of I and you as in "I'm only trying to help you" or "I'll take your word for it."

The Pleaser

The Pleaser's intention is to please others. He will stop, reflect, and explore issues and understand events. It's a speculative style, characterized by the following behaviors:

Giving impressions: "Sometimes I get the impression you're preoccupied with other things."
Giving explanations: "I usually do that when I'm uncertain. Do you know what I mean?"
Expressing deference: "I'll do whatever you would like to do."
Asking for opinions: "What do you think I should do?"
Referring to others: "The marketing department used this program, and so should we."

Encouraging feedback: "How do you see this situation?"
Reflecting: "It seems to me you've really been working hard lately."
Making "one down" statements: "Do you think we could set aside
  some time to talk today?" (Nunally, Miller, and Wackman, 1975)

Characteristic language includes qualifiers (such as probably, maybe, sometimes, perhaps, hopefully, could, might) and qualified self-disclosures ("I probably was mad at you just then.") When he focuses on an important issue, the Pleaser usually handles it in a safe way, often discussing past events or possible future events. There is little self-disclosure and no commitment to take action to do something about any issue. In short, the Pleaser typically expresses a commitment to deal with an issue, but there is little commitment to take any type of action (Nunally, Miller, and Wackman, 1975).

The Pleaser experiences a low sense of self-worth and has not learned the art of assertiveness. The Pleaser usually avoids interaction and as a result experiences a self-fulfilling prophecy. As the Pleaser avoids interaction, he or she also avoids opportunities to become known to others. In the end, the Pleaser actually is avoided and his or her goals are not met either.

The Influencer

The Influencer wants to deal with an issue rather than avoid it. This style involves being in touch with one's feelings and the actions of others as well as being responsible for oneself. Statements such as "You're making me" or "You cause me to" shift responsibility to another and are not used in this style. The Influencer's behavior is the outcome of the sensitive attitude.

The Influencer is self-aware and discloses that awareness, while trying to understand others. The Influencer provides an atmosphere of caring and mutual support. Some examples of the Influencer's communication behavior include:

Speaking for self: "I've been doing some thinking about it and I don't
  want to miss this opportunity."
Interpreting others' reactions: "I'm sensing you're apprehensive
  about this move."
Making interpretations: "What I hear you saying is that you are opposed to the idea; am I correct?"
Sharing feelings: "I am uncomfortable defending this issue."
Making intentions clear: "I will support the move all the way."
Making action statements: "I am voting for the move."
Double-checking: "So far we have two opposed and two for the
  move; is that correct?"

Asking for acknowledgment: "I'd like to go ahead with the move if
the two of you agree it's the best for us."
Acknowledging the other: "You have every right to feel that way."
Confirming, clarifying: "That is a valuable contribution; would you
care to apply that to our next major decision?"
(Nunally, Miller, and Wackman, 1975)

When you use this style effectively, it is accompanied by an attitude of
allowing yourself and another to grow. Your tone of voice, what you say,
your body posture, and your facial gestures all can be cues to the spirit behind
what's being said.

The Influencer grew up in an open and supportive environment. He
or she was encouraged to make his or her own decisions and was given
freedom to explore the environment. He or she is likely to take responsibility
for personal actions and intentions. The Influencer style is important to effective communication. It is also the most effective way to deal with important relationship issues. In short, each style plays an important role in effective
and flexible communication.

Using Knowledge of the Styles

The effective communicator is flexible. She or he recognizes the differences in styles, can monitor his or her own style of communication, and is
able to use different styles appropriately to express different intentions. No
single style can be used to effectively communicate all the different intentions a person has. A flexible, effective communicator understands this and
matches style with intentions.

It is possible to observe these communication styles in the workplace,
particularly in the way managers or superiors relate to subordinates. There
is a direct relationship between one's communication style and the type of
work one chooses. In a study conducted at the University of Colorado,
Boulder, it was found that the majority of the school's administrators are
Directors. The majority of social service workers are Helpers, while Pleasers
tend to choose careers that require little interaction—and even choose to sit
in locations where there is minimal chance of contact and visibility (Harvey,
1970).

Many hasty employment decisions could be made more wisely simply
by paying attention to communication styles. One would certainly not want
a Director as a secretary. In selecting a safety manager or marketing representative, one would find that an Influencer would be well suited to the job.

Table 1.2 summarizes each communication style in chart form. The
following chart, Table 1.3, presents tips for managing each type of style.

Table 1.2   Style Summary

Communication Style	Preferred Working Environment	Use of Time	
		Priorities	Pace
Player	Safe Friendly Casual	Create a positive impression	Leisurely
Director	Task- oriented	Efficiency Effectiveness	Quick Controlled
Helper	Friendly	Assisting others	Lesiurely Ordered
Pleaser	Cooperative Friendly	Relationship before task	Leisurely Deliberate
Influencer	Enthusiastic Open Flexible	Flexible agenda	Quick Undisciplined

Table 1.3   Managing the Styles

Communication Style	Information to Share	To Win Acceptance	Solving Problems	Making Decisions
Player	Current events Timely news Feedback Compliments	Give personal attention and support	Help identify real issues and options	Offer encourage- ment Encourage risk taking
Director	Expressions of credibility and confidence	Show evidence of ability to get re- sults	Give complete responsibility of task and support conclusions	Provide options Give probabili- ties
Helper	Feedback Appreciation	Give recognition and ensure credit	Help identify long-term goals and steps needed to get there	Offer encourage- ment Give personal assurances and guarantees
Pleaser	Evidence of trustworthiness Openness Common interests	Give personal attention and admiration	Support feelings Show interest in the relationship	Offer opinions Give personal assurances and guarantees
Influencer	Personal observations Self-disclosure	Give recognition Emphasize what's in it for him/her or the company	Support his/her ideas, opin- ions, dreams Show interest in the relationship	Give testimony and incentives for risking quick actions

COMMUNICATION GAMES

At this point, let us review. We have characterized three communication attitudes. We have described five communication styles that stem from these attitudes. While you may find it easy to categorize others you know, it is important to keep in mind that most people change their attitudes and communication behaviors for different situations. When a person does not change his or her attitude or style, we consider the person to be stuck in a particular style. In such a situation, it is important that one break out of a ritualized style and increase awareness of the self and the situation one is in to more appropriately respond for better results.

According to Virginia Satir, author of *Peoplemaking* (1972), when a person is under stress and is experiencing a low sense of self-worth, it is quite likely that communication games are being played. Satir further states that most of the time a person is unaware that a game is being played. Games are being played when a person's body language and nonverbal messages don't agree with the spoken message. When under stress a person will act differently from usual and will respond as though he or she feels unimportant.

Satir presents four games people play when they feel this way: Placating, Blaming, Computing, and Distracting. By playing any of these four games, we can escape the possibility of being rejected by the person we are communicating with, as shown in the following statements:

- We placate so that the other will not become upset.
- We blame so the other will assume we are strong.
- We can compute to sound reasonable and intelligent.
- We can be distracting and not respond to the situation or the other directly.

Let's explore each of Satir's games.

Placating

The Placator is your typical "Yes man" who tries to please and apologize, and who never disagrees. He or she feels responsible for all that happens and agrees with personal criticism made by others. The Placator will say "Yes" no matter what he or she may think or feel.

Placating messages:

"Whatever you want is fine with me, as long as you're happy."
(Supervisor to employee) "I'm, uh, uh, gee, Jim, I am sorry, I don't want to upset you, no, you're doing OK, it's just, maybe you could try a little harder, just a little, huh?"

Blaming

The Blamer finds fault, dictates, and bosses, and is interested in throwing his weight around. With feelings of low self-worth, the blamer tries to get others to obey so he or she feels important.

Blaming messages:

"You never do anything right. What's the matter with you?"
(Supervisor to employee) "For God's sake, man, don't you know anything? Who hired you in the first place?"

Computing

The Computer refrains from showing feelings, acting calm and collected. He or she uses the longest words possible to try to appear intelligent.

Computing messages:

"If one were to observe carefully, one might notice the work-worn hands of someone present here."
(Supervisor to employee) "We are doing a survey of our organization's efficiency. We find that in this department, namely, with you, that efficiency is beginning to degrade. Do you have any justification which might put this into perspective?"

Distracting

The Distractor makes very little sense, seldom responds to the point, and typically ignores questions by answering a different question.

Distracting messages:

(Employee) "Could you please do something about my work station; it is always so overcrowded with equipment and hard to move around in."
(Distracting supervisor) "Work stations around here have never had proper equipment. I like those new instruments by ABC Corp."

For Satir (1972), all of these games lack clarity in communication. She says they are games because someone usually loses in the process and it's usually the game player.

HEALTHY COMMUNICATION

For years, communication theorists and practitioners have distinguished between healthy and unhealthy communication. Table 1.4 exemplifies the distinction.

Table 1.4   Healthy and Unhealthy Communication

Healthy	Unhealthy
Speaking for self	Blaming
Feelings	Placating
Intentions	Computing
Actions	Distracting
Checking perceptions	Ignoring
Asking for feedback	Interrupting
Confirming others	Disconfirming
Cooperating	Aggressive
	Competitive
Being clear and concise	Ambiguous
Self-disclosing	Guarded
Being spontaneous	Strategic
Accepting	Evaluating
Examples: "Jim, your work area needs improvement. You haven't straightened it up since last week. We need to take a look to see what's wrong."	"Jim, you're so sloppy. Maybe you should tell me what your problem is with picking up at your station."

A good formula to use for healthy communication in problem situations is to structure the message as follows: "I feel/think _____, when you/we _____, because _____." Example: "I think it is counterproductive when we argue over whose plan is better because I am willing to make whatever change is necessary to make things work out."

Through the use of healthy communication, relationships can exist without threat to either person's self-esteem. In healthy communication you are aware of what you are doing and prepared to face the consequences for your actions. In healthy communication, feelings are shown freely and non-verbal communication matches the verbal communictaion. Communication is clear and straightforward. This promotes trust, because others know where they stand and feel good in your presence.

Our research suggests that there are few companies that reward healthy communication. Yet we know that employees long for straightforward, honest, and open communication. Simply using healthy communication can improve morale and improve working relationships. Others will usually follow the example because it feels good.

Satir has found that on the average, for any group of people:

50 percent will say yes no matter what they feel

30 percent will say no regardless of the subject

15 percent will say neither yes nor no and give no indication of their feelings

.50 percent will behave as though yes or no did not exist

4.50 percent will respond in a straightforward manner

(Satir, 1972, p. 78)

An effective manager's job is to help others feel it is safe to express ideas and feelings through his or her own communication behavior.

2

The Communication Process ▲

A MODEL OF COMMUNICATION

The most practical definition of communication is the elicitation of a response. When we communicate, we try to influence another to respond to our words in some way. The only way to know if we have communicated effectively is to determine whether we achieved the response we desired. For this reason, effective communication is defined as eliciting a desired response.

Communication is a dynamic, ongoing process. It includes the elements of feedback, feed forward, the environment, and frames of reference for both the sender and receiver. Sender and receiver are mutual and reciprocal; they affect each other.

Figure 2.1   The Communication Model

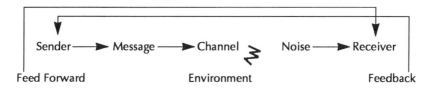

Frame of Reference

The key to effective communication and receiving your desired response is to consider the interaction of all the variables. Each variable has an impact on the others. If you don't consider how they simultaneously interact, you can easily focus too much on one variable, impeding effective communication. Let's consider the primary components of the communication process and what happens when you neglect to consider all of them together and instead concentrate on one specific variable.

Sender

Oftentimes we encounter communication problems when the sender considers self as the primary tool. Effectiveness for the sender-centered communicator becomes the simple act of transmitting the message and relieving the desire to communicate. A sender-centered individual assumes there is only one way to express a thought. Such an individual talks *to or at* others, because the primary focal point is the self. The sender is concerned only with the message and fails to consider (1) the most effective way to phrase the message, (2) the appropriate channel, and (3) the receiver's needs at that particular moment. As a result, the sender-centered communicator frequently interrupts others with inappropriately phrased messages that are not always related to events at hand. In safety management, one of the prime determinants of the sender's effectiveness is the receiver's perception of the sender's credibility.

Channel

In other situations the channel becomes the primary tool. Try to recall a situation where the person you have communicated with said "Remember the meeting when we discussed . . ." These channel-centered individuals communicate from a limited perspective where the communication event is paramount. They only need to verify with others that a certain subject was discussed to engage in their usual "I told you so" or "It's right here on this memo" routines. While in many respects, the medium is the message (McLuhan, 1964), other aspects of the communication model are equally important in determining effectiveness.

Message

The message itself is important in determining communication effectiveness. Communication is the means by which people influence one another. It involves sorting, selecting, and sending symbols to enable the receiver to recreate in his mind the intended meaning. Meaning lies not just in the words we use, but also in nonverbal gestures, tone of voice, facial expression, and the setting. In other words, how we interact determines the real meaning of our communication.

People who center on the sender, message, or channel create problems because they fail to consider where meaning is established. Meaning is not transmitted; it is shared in a process and is ultimately determined by the receiver of the message. Those who share messages adapted to the needs of the receiver are usually better communicators and experience fewer communication breakdowns.

Receiver

While we have advocated the need to consider the receiver when communicating, a receiver-centered communicator carried to the extreme also creates problems. The sender may simply reflect what the receiver wishes to hear and what the situation calls for. The result: no real contribution is made by the sender. Such an approach is seen in performance evaluations when a supervisor tries not to discourage the employee and says "You are doing just fine." It also occurs when two people who want desperately to please each other carry on a conversation to the extreme of asking, "What do you want to do?" with the reply, "I don't know, what do you want to do?"

Feedback

When managers look at the goals of their communication, they begin to realize how important feedback is to them. If an employee agrees to complete a report on production problems, the verbal agreement signifies immediately that the communication requesting the report is effective. However, as the deadline approaches the manager cannot know whether the report contains the desired information or is even started without a progress report. A feedback-centered manager always solicits immediate feedback at the time the message is conveyed and monitors progress by establishing times when interim feedback is due, indicating stages of completion. The feedback you receive is the only way to determine whether your message is effective. Feedback is the determinant of effective communication.

Problems do occur, however, with feedback-centered people. For example, the feedback-centered manager utilizes feedback to monitor effectiveness. The all-encompassing question becomes: "Are you getting the job done?" Such persistence may lead employees to believe the manager regards them only as cogs in a machine rather than as the humans they are. The feedback-centered manager's concern for effectiveness can distort the process and adversely affect the feelings of the receivers involved.

The key to successful communication is realizing that the method of communication is just as important as achieving the goal of communication. The process (interaction of all variables) must be recognized to ensure quality communication.

THE PROCESS OF ORGANIZING AND COMMUNICATION

Communication is what permits people to organize. It permits people to coordinate their activities to accomplish common objectives. But there is more to communication than a mere transmission of information or transfer of meaning. People form their view of reality and develop personal expectations through the exchange of symbols.

For example, Mrs. Jones asks her secretary to make ten copies of a report and distribute them among the members of her department. Mrs. Jones expects from previous experience with the secretary that this person will (1) understand the instructions, (2) be willing to carry them out, and (3) perform the task with reasonable accuracy and speed. Mrs. Jones's behavior is based on her expectations about the secretary's behavior. When Mrs. Jones holds a staff meeting, she will expect her staff to be familiar with the content of that report since she will assume it has been distributed and read. It is only when expectations are shared that coordination is possible and organizing takes place. When meanings and expectations are not shared, individuals simply function in their own private worlds, doing their own things, uninvolved with others and unpredictable to others.

As indicated earlier, communication occupies a central place in organizations. Communication is the binding element that keeps the various interdependent parts of the organizational system together. Communication allows organizations to develop by giving separate individuals the means to coordinate their activities and thus achieve common goals.

Organizations are not as much structures as they are activities. It is more accurate to speak of organizing than of organizations, because organizations are something that people accomplish through a process. People act in such a way that their behaviors are interlocked. One person's behavior is contingent on another's, and for the activities to interlock, there must be communication. Organizing is accomplished through processes that are developed to deal with uncertainty. Communication serves to achieve a common meaning among group members, which is the mechanism by which uncertainty is reduced.

Our environment is rapidly and constantly changing. A total lack of organizational change means stagnation for the system. It seems critical that organizational systems and subsystems adapt effectively to change. The more change that occurs, the greater the need exists for effective communication. People increase their communication to cope with changes around them. People are open to change until they reach a point where they no longer can cope. Once that point is reached, they remove themselves from the change or distort the situation and fight the change. Organizations, as do people, have certain limits on the amount of change they can handle. Perhaps that is why most organizations attempt to restrict change. It is easier to restrict change than it is to fight the consequences of it.

ORGANIZATIONAL COMMUNICATION

It is possible that an organization can negatively affect our communication skills. Such organizations value productivity and rationality rather than clear communication. According to a noted management theorist, this forces us to hide our feelings and, as a result, experience difficulty in expressing our feelings and ideas (Argyris, 1962).

Communication skills become strained because we learn to hide our feelings, withhold feedback, and build our defenses. These behaviors prevent openness to new ideas, risk taking, and task creativity. The result is a decrease in an organization's capacity to experiment and try new ideas. In so doing, the organization loses its vitality. The ultimate result is organizational confusion. That's when employees begin to ask themselves, "Why are people behaving that way toward me?" or, "Why do they interpret me incorrectly?" This happens because we can't predict what influence we have on others.

In order to maintain a sense of self-esteem, employees begin to question the honesty and genuineness of fellow workers, which in turn leads to frustration and feelings of failure with regard to relationships. Such behavior further generates mistrust and the tendency to "play it safe" and "say the right thing" in order to feel accepted. Organizations achieve employee commitment through power (the capacity to direct, reward, and penalize), control, mistrust, and conformity, all of which create employee defensiveness and eventually lead to less effective leadership by management (Argyris, 1962). When executives perceive that their leadership is not as effective as they would wish, they then emphasize more productivity and begin checking employees' work. They try to manage by questioning employees, which makes the workers feel even more defensive. This is also known as "management by crisis." In addition, in such situations management may be unclear in giving explanations or may fail to offer employees recognition and support.

Organizations need to focus on improving communication skills over and above technical skills, job design, management controls, incentive systems, or any modification of values. Should an organization promote communication skills, the impact made on employees would be tremendous.

In an organization, communicating involves several other variables that tend to inhibit effective interpersonal communication. Looking at these variables helps determine why communication is a major organizational problem and how such problems might be resolved. When we are communicating, it is easy to operate under a number of organizational assumptions that actually inhibit effective communication. Listed below are just a few.

We assume that

- We have little effect upon others.
- Conflict is bad.
- People are perfect communicators.
- Communication is separate from management.
- Life is fair and organizations are fair.
- When we're given a job to do, we are in control.

Let's examine these assumptions one by one.

We have little effect upon others.

Working in a large company can make a person feel alienated and unimportant. Actually, through the use of good communication skills we can have tremendous impact on others in the organization.

Conflict is bad.

We tend to avoid conflict, and while doing so, risk stagnating rather than changing and growing. As presented later in this text, conflict generates information and growth.

People are perfect communicators.

There is no such thing as a perfect communicator. Good communication comes with training. The ability to be an effective communicator is not innate.

Communication is separate from management.

Managing is a process of influencing others, and that influence occurs through communication. For managers, communicating fills the majority of their time. They listen, question, and seek feedback, and when action is decided upon, they need to gain support. Communication is central to a manager's activities. In other words, management is communication.

Life is fair and organizations are fair.

Fairness is a concept, not a condition that always prevails. To expect fairness only leads to disillusionment. By practicing good communication skills, we can grow and learn to take responsibility for that which we expect. Most people operate on a value-for-value exchange basis. In other words, as long as we receive equal to the amount we give, we feel a sense of fairness. If this is not the case, we do have a choice as to how much inequity we will accept (Adams, 1963).

Picture two scales that are in balance. Now picture the scale with one side lower than the other. Perhaps an employee feels his or her efforts are greater than the efforts of other employees who are paid more. Seeing less value received than given, the employee will probably do one of the following:

- Decrease his amount of effort commensurate with the perceived inequity in pay.
- Ask for a raise.
- Look for another job.
- Call in sick.
- Assume management doesn't care.
- Steal office products in attempt to increase value received.

As long as the scales are equal, the employee and boss will be relatively satisfied and work motivation will continue.

When we're given a job to do, we are in control.

Too often we simply agree to the demands placed upon us. Too seldom do we question the reasons for completing a task and the value it represents to the company. By such questioning, we can gain more information and satisfaction with the job we are expected to perform, and we can perform it more successfully.

KEY STEPS FOR IMPROVING ORGANIZATIONAL COMMUNICATION

Remember the importance of the spoken word.

It is important to make that which you expect known to others. In other words, make the unstated stated. If you don't, there is no one to blame for unmet expectations but yourself.

Strive to achieve functional information.

Strive for shared meaning with the person to whom you are communicating. Functional information is information you both agree upon and perceive in the same way. As long as both parties perceive the meaning of flex-time in the same way, for example, there will be clear communication of what work hours are acceptable. If one employee views flex-time as coming and going as you please while the other sees it as a flexible start and stop time that is stable and agreed upon in advance, meaning will not be shared, and expectations will be violated.

Ask for more information.

By doing so, you gain more satisfaction and more information, which benefits both yourself and the person with whom you are communicating.

Be receiver-centered.

By doing so you can communicate more effectively and adapt what you have to say for the person with whom you are speaking.

Check your perceptions.

When you are in doubt, check it out. Perceptions can be deceiving and can lead to problems if they are not checked.

Focus on the needs of employees.

Compliance with any order is more likely when needs are considered. For example, employees want to know what management expects of them, to have enough information to get the job done, to be recognized for their work, and to be considered significant contributors to the organization. Frequently managers misunderstand or fail to consider these needs. Managers may mistakenly send incomplete information in their instructions. As a result, workers misinterpret the message. The employee's behavior probably shows a lack of interest in the manager's message, which causes the manager to criticize the employee for not being fully involved on the job or, worse yet, for not doing the job right.

Solicit and receive communication and feedback from employees.

How does a manager determine the extent of the employees' needs in order to frame the messages? Quite simply, managers must receive communication and feedback from employees. Knowing what the needs are and knowing how to develop them for each employee are two different issues. To develop messages that employees comply with, managers must understand employees through communication with them. Getting the employee to talk with the manager freely and accurately is no easy matter. Employees fail to communicate with a manager because they fear that expressing their true feelings about the company to their boss could be dangerous. Employees are not likely to communicate upward at all. However, when they do, they distort information to please managers, telling them what they want to know.

Develop a trusting, supportive climate.

To encourage upward communication, the manager must meet certain employee needs. Employees need (1) to know what is expected of them, (2) to possess information needed to get the job done, (3) to be evaluated and recognized for work completed, and (4) to understand their value to the organization. You can achieve this by treating employees as important people, as you expect to be treated. Take time to manage by walking around (Peters and Waterman, 1982). In other words, walk down the halls or to the lunch room and talk with employees. This encourages them to feel more free to talk. Whether the information you receive is positive or not, the way you respond to the information will determine how trusting and supportive the work climate is.

Strive for quality relationships.

The quality of the superior-subordinate relationship is the most important contributor to job satisfaction. In a high-quality relationship the superior praises the subordinate, understands the subordinate's job, trusts and can be trusted, exudes warmth, demonstrates honesty, and encourages subordinates to disagree.

Develop realistic expectations.

We often expect more from others than they can give. You can realize or adjust your expectations by exercising control of the communication process. Skill in communication provides you the opportunity to question, determine the person's position, and find the information necessary to proceed realistically within the organization.

Refine your communication skills.

Senior managers expect to see skills in interpersonal relations in employees. When asked to consider the importance of various skills, they consistently ranked communication as number one—over the ability to motivate, utilize work skills, plan, develop, coordinate, analyze, make decisions, and utilize a computer. Employees face the responsibility of communicating with others on the job to ensure coordination and cooperation with superiors. The responsibility is not a light one. It requires considerable care in developing communication patterns with other employees and management.

Provide feedback to management.

Senior managers are not always available because of work responsibilities that must be met. Likewise, they are not always ready to deal with matters employees wish to discuss. With the influential factors of status, power, routine work, work overload, ambiguous jurisdiction, and so forth, the feedback task becomes complex and difficult to implement. Despite the seemingly numerous barriers employees face in maintaining relationships, they must begin by initiating feedback to management.

While communicating to management may seem to be an impossible task, certain information indicates that this task can be successful if the following principles are respected:

1. Make communication positive, and it is more likely to be used by top decision makers.
2. Make communication timely, and it is more likely to be used by top management.
3. Communication is more likely to be accepted if it supports current policy.
4. Communication is more likely to be effective if it goes directly to the person who can act on it.
5. Communication is more effective when it has intuitive appeal for the receiver.

(Koehler and Huber, 1976)

Ask for information and check your perceptions.

The skill critical to improving work relationships in any job is checking one's perceptions and inferences for accuracy. When doubts or uncertainties arise, the employee benefits by realizing who risks most by not clarifying. When managers are misinterpreted they typically issue blame on those persons who misinterpret. By acquiring the requisite information necessary to prevent misinterpretation, employees benefit the most.

THE IMPORTANCE OF CLIMATE

Much has been written on the topic of how an organization's climate and culture affect employee participation and performance. In general, the communication climate is the sum total of how individuals relate to one another in an organization. It is determined partly by the norms and values that all members believe in and partly by policies and procedures, but mostly by the quality of day-to-day interaction between boss and subordinate and between peers.

A healthy climate encourages open, two-way communication and promotes motivation and satisfaction. The healthy climate can be recognized by the prevalence of individuals practicing the skills outlined in the previous pages. It takes a great amount of energy and practice to keep a climate healthy. Such a task warrants day-to-day investment of personal time and priorities.

In an unhealthy climate, distrust, suspicion, fear, and provincialism are the norm. People are afraid to speak up and suggest improvements. The newspapers are full of stories in which employees were unable to effectively communicate their safety concerns to management and felt compelled to take the information to the media, where they felt more attention would be paid. An unhealthy climate sets the stage for blocking important information from getting to the most effective place and for frustrated employees to look for ways other than the chain of command to make change happen. The questionnaire in Figure 2.2 will help you assess the climate in your organization.

PRESCRIPTION FOR A HEALTHY CLIMATE

If you characterize your company as having an unhealthy climate, you have at least three choices: put up with it, make a difference, or get out. To make a difference, nothing is more effective than leading by example. Identify the aspects about the climate that contribute to unhealthy behavior and refuse to participate in them. Make a conscious effort to promote open and honest communication in your own dealings and watch how quickly others respond to you. While you may sense some resistance at first, keep in mind that you are changing the rules about how people relate to one another by your behavior. Also recognize that people prefer to be treated with respect and need to be affirmed in their communication. The positive messages and approaches you instigate will overwhelm negative habits, because you will eventually receive support from others.

Figure 2.2   How's Your Communication Climate?

Answer the following questions by circling the response that most closely describes the climate in your workplace: (A)lways,(F)requently, (O)ccasionally, (S)eldom, (N)ever

A   F   O   S   N   1. There is not much need to keep secrets around here.

A   F   O   S   N   2. I can be open and honest when talking with my boss, even when the news is negative.

A   F   O   S   N   3. I generally hear about company problems from management before I hear about it from friends or the news media.

A   F   O   S   N   4. When an associate or subordinate comes to me with a suggestion about how I could improve my performance, I am generally willing to listen and be open-minded.

A   F   O   S   N   5. I can mention sensitive issues with my associates without the fear of taking the wrong position or looking incompetent.

A   F   O   S   N   6. When I present a new idea or a suggestion for improving operations, it is welcomed and acted upon by management.

A   F   O   S   N   7. My career success is a result of mutual planning and expectations with my boss rather than who I know.

A   F   O   S   N   8. People are generally treated as professionals around here.

A   F   O   S   N   9. Bad news is generally accepted; there's a real effort to understand and problem solve rather than to blame and dispense retribution.

A   F   O   S   N   10. It's easy to tell how management views your performance around here, even when you know it's good.

A   F   O   S   N   11. Suggestions and complaints are acted on and responded to by upper management.

A   F   O   S   N   12. We're encouraged to think about the company's and the community's best interests first and not view the needs of our department as the main consideration.

A   F   O   S   N   13. The way to get ahead around here is to help others succeed.

A   F   O   S   N   14. Everyone is treated as an equal contributor around here, from upper management through the hourly employees.

A   F   O   S   N   15. Superior performance is expected and rewarded.

If your responded (S)eldom or (N)ever to any of the above questions, those items may suggest problems in the communication climate of your company.

SUMMARY

Successful organizational communicators are those who understand how communication levels and processes affect their relationships with others. No matter where one is stationed in an organization and what skills one possesses, attention to communication is paramount if the individual is to be successful and the organization is to be effective and efficient. Understanding the levels of communication, the process of communication, and how the process functions places a considerable burden on every organizational communicator. Awareness and mastery of the process, the interpersonal variables affecting the process, and the skills necessary to meet the demands are only the beginning steps. Successful interpersonal communication demands a daily commitment to the process.

3
Motivating through Communication ▲

COMMUNICATION AS A MANAGEMENT TOOL

If communication is eliciting a response, then effective communication can be defined as eliciting the desired response, as stated in Chapter 2. You attempt to get what you want using words and actions. You can determine whether your communication is effective by the response you receive. The clearer you are in expressing your message, the more likely you are to get the response you want. In this chapter we will explore communication techniques that motivate employees. Key management skills include giving clear instructions, building trust and power, calibrating disclosure, active listening, and using expectations to motivate employees.

Most management schools offer little training in communication skills. As a result, most managers enter their positions unprepared to do their jobs successfully and later wonder why they aren't getting the results they desire. Management theorists contend that most of today's managers have been "miseducated"; they don't take enough interest in their people, and as a result they have become isolated. A big contributing factor is the lack of communication skills. Peters and Waterman, authors of *In Search of Excellence*, state that the number one productivity problem in America is managers who are out of touch with their people (1982).

As indicated in the first chapter, over 25 studies reveal that communication skills are the most important single factor in determining managerial success, above accounting, financial, or computer skills. These studies suggest that communication skills are indispensable to managers. The College Placement Council survey showed the following results (Goldhaber, 1979, p. 143):

Skills identified as most important to success (regardless of field) after:

One year on the job	Communication
Seven years on the job	Communication
Ten years on the job	Communication

Skills most important to success according to various occupations:

Office worker	Written communication
Mathematician	Written communication
Scientist	Written communication
Engineer	Written communication
Administrator	Written communication
Salesperson	Oral communication
Health worker	Oral communication
Educator	Oral communication
Social worker	Oral communication
Counselor	Oral communication

The *Harvard Business Review* survey (Bowman, 1964, p. 14) placed in rank order the most important characteristics of a promotable executive. The results are as follows:

1. Ability to communicate
2. Ambition
3. Education
4. Capacity for hard work

The American Business Communication Association survey of one hundred companies showed how managers spend time (Wyllie, 1980). The results, in percentages, are as follows:

80%	Interviewing
78%	Verbal communication with subordinates
76%	Oral reports
75%	Communication with clients

The Colorado State University Engineering College study gave the following results (Muchinsky, 1974) concerning the rank order of classes important for success on the job:

1. Public speaking
2. Group siscussion
3. Technical communication
4. Senior engineering design

Clearly, in addition to task competence, managers must also have people competence. The average executive spends 75 to 80 percent of his or her time on the job communicating with others. It is ironic that managers spend so much of their time communicating, while communication skills are consistently listed as the number one weakness of today's managers. This weakness is not always the manager's fault. The way many organizations are structured tends to create communication problems. Rapid growth and change also creates problems. As a result, communication becomes strained, conformity is demanded, values are altered, and employees spend more time adjusting to change than they do producing. Managers rely more on the formal hierarchy to get results than on their own ability to influence. The result: communication is ineffective and the expectations placed on managers are impossible. Excellence in communication requires listening, trust, and respect for each person in the organization.

If you are a manager, you probably spend more time communicating than you do in the classical management functions of planning, organizing, directing, and controlling. The terms "manage" and "management" would best be discarded and replaced with "leading," which connotes unleashing energy, building, and fostering growth rather than controlling, reducing, and arranging. Peters and Waterman, authors of *In Search of Excellence* (1982), assert that an effective manager coaches and orchestrates his or her staff. You can only do this through face-to-face communication, through helping people to reach their peak performance. Things are accomplished through people.

USING COMMUNICATION TECHNIQUES TO IMPROVE PERFORMANCE

Your ability to motivate requires competence in interpersonal communication skills, which we might call key management skills. Your employees are motivated by your enthusiasm, consistent expectations, recognition of performance, accessibility and willingness to listen, openness about company information, risk taking, skill in dealing with mistakes, and sensitivity to others. In order to improve employee motivation, you need to enhance your employees' self-esteem, treat them as individuals, and show that you trust them.

By considering what employees want, you are better able to meet their needs and improve their motivation, performance, and productivity. Most employees want to fit in and to be stars (Peters and Waterman, 1982). Most love praise and want to think of themselves as winners. Employees also need meaning in their life and will sacrifice a great deal to an organization that provides it for them. They have a need to feel in charge of their job. They thrive on independence with a moderate amount of support, direction, and positive feedback. Using rewards, celebrating success, recognizing achievement, and creating some degree of competition increases performance and makes employees feel like stars. Involving employees in decisions, informing them of current news, using employee suggestions—all help to make people feel they are important to the company. Employees want recognition, communication with management, and information on why a job needs to be done. They need feedback and a feeling of belonging.

ACTIVE LISTENING

According to one communication scientist, we spend 70 percent of our day communicating, and 45 percent of this time is spent listening . Yet the average worker typically retains only 50 percent of what is heard. Two weeks later, only 25 percent is retained (Nichols and Stevens, 1957, pp. 1–17).

The following listening studies yielded interesting information.

Average white collar worker	Listening efficiency
After ten minute presentation	50% retention
After 48 hours	25% retention

(Nichols and Stevens, 1957)

Time spent in communication for senior and midlevel managers:

Listening	32.7%
Speaking	25.8%
Writing	22.6%
Reading	18.8%

(Kotter, 1982)

Academy of Certified Administrative Managers survey—skills most crucial for managerial ability:

1. Active listening (super critical rating)

2. Listening

(Becker and Eckdom, 1980)

College Placement Council survey—skills managers wished had been offered in college:

1. Listening

2. Interpersonal skills

(DiSalvo, Larsen, and Seiler, 1976)

Opinion Research Corporation—main complaint of subordinates about management:

1. Supervisors don't listen to them

(Dover, 1958, pp. 269–275)

Think of someone you consider a good communicator, and you will probably find a good listener. Listening is the most important skill in human communication. And listening skills can have dramatic bottom-line impact. Figure 3.1 is a short quiz to assess your listening skills and attitudes.

Figure 3.1   Listening Skills Assessment

Answer the following true-false questions regarding the listening process. The answers appear after the quiz.

T _____	F _____	1. Speaking is a more important part of the communication process than listening.
T _____	F _____	2. Since listening requires little energy, it is very easy.
T _____	F _____	3. Listening is an automatic, involuntary reflex.
T _____	F _____	4. Speakers can make listening occur in an audience.
T _____	F _____	5. The terms "hearing ability" and "listening ability" can be used interchangeably.
T _____	F _____	6. When they need to, people can force themselves to listen well.
T _____	F _____	7. The speaker is primarily responsible for the success of communication.
T _____	F _____	8. People listen every day. This daily practice eliminates the need for listening training.
T _____	F _____	9. Competence in listening develops naturally.
T _____	F _____	10. When you learned to read, you simultaneously learned to listen.
T _____	F _____	11. Listening is only a matter of understanding the words of the speaker.
T _____	F _____	12. People remember most of what they hear.
T _____	F _____	13. Although you may not listen well all the time, when you need to or want to, you can turn your listening ability on and listen well.
T _____	F _____	14. Your listening cannot be improved.
T _____	F _____	15. Attitudes are unrelated to listening.
T _____	F _____	16. Memory and listening are the same thing.
T _____	F _____	17. You listen as well as you will ever be able to.
T _____	F _____	18. Listening is influenced primarily by intelligence.
T _____	F _____	19. Your listening and reading vocabularies are identical.
T _____	F _____	20. Listening habits cannot be changed.

Answers to the Quiz

All of the statements were false. If you marked one or more true, you should gain a deeper understanding of the listening process, particularly of the role of active listening during communication. If you marked all of the answers false, congratulations! You are already aware of some basic principles concerning listening that many people do not recognize.

The next quiz, Figure 3.2, helps you determine whether or not you are a good listener.

Figure 3.2   Are You a Good Listener?

Attitudes	Almost Always	Usually	Occasionally	Seldom	Almost Never
1. Do you like to listen to other people talk?	5	4	3	2	1
2. Do you encourage others to talk?	5	4	3	2	1
3. Do you listen even if you do not like the person who is talking?	5	4	3	2	1
4. Do you listen equally well whether the person talking is man or woman, young or old?	5	4	3	2	1
5. Do you listen equally well to friend, acquaintance, stranger?	5	4	3	2	1
Actions					
6. Do you put what you have been doing out of sight and out of mind?	5	4	3	2	1
7. Do you look at the speaker?	5	4	3	2	1
8. Do you ignore distractions?	5	4	3	2	1
9. Do you smile, nod your head, and otherwise encourage the speaker?	5	4	3	2	1
10. Do you think about what she is saying?	5	4	3	2	1
11. Do you try to figure out what he means?	5	4	3	2	1

12. Do you try to figure out why she is saying it?	5	4	3	2	1
13. Do you let him finish what he is trying to say?	5	4	3	2	1
14. If she hesitates, do you encourage her to go on?	5	4	3	2	1
15. Do you restate what he has said and ask him if you got it right?	5	4	3	2	1
16. Do you withhold judgment about her idea until she has finished?	5	4	3	2	1
17. Do you listen regardless of his manner of speaking and choice of words?	5	4	3	2	1
18. Do you listen even though you anticipate what she is going to say?	5	4	3	2	1
19. Do you question him in order to get him to explain his idea more fully?	5	4	3	2	1
20. Do you ask her what the words mean?	5	4	3	2	1

Poor listening is one of the primary causes of managerial and clerical error. Each error that needs correcting means costs in letter writing, phone calls, personnel time, machine time, materials, lost orders, or missed deadlines. Major organizations such as 3M, AT&T, General Electric, and Dunn and Bradstreet include listening in their training. Xerox's program for improving listening has been used by over 1.5 million employees in 71,000 companies. Sperry Corporation invested more than $4 million to set up listening seminars for its 87,000 employees. (Adler, 1983)

The reasons for poor listening are many. Most of us have developed poor listening habits. Some of us could be called pseudolisteners who act as if we are listening, or fake it. Some of us may be selective listeners who listen only for what interests us. The defensive listener listens only for personal attacks and ignores the rest. The insensitive listener listens only to the words used rather than the entire message and takes remarks at face value, ignoring other subtleties. In general, we all tend to dismiss that which is uninteresting, focus on the delivery of the message, and yield to distractions rather than truly listen.

Several factors affect listening. We usually listen more intently to agreeable topics. We listen more closely when there's something in it for ourselves, when there's a good reason to listen. In addition to preference and motivation, personality, location, and societal roles affect our listening behavior.

Nonattending or pseudolistening behavior often communicates disinterest, boredom, disagreement, or even hostility. The irony of poor listening is that many times we do not intend to communicate such impressions. Yet when we are silent, unresponsive listeners, our nonattending behaviors communicate to others intentions very different from our real ones. To overcome these natural obstacles, when you are a listener, try to identify the speaker's main ideas and keep your own in the background. Be ready to listen by facing the speaker squarely. Uncross your arms, lean forward, maintain eye contact, and be relaxed.

Your ability to listen is also determined by your acceptance of the speaker. Listening means understanding what is being said by the other person, even if you do not agree with the other's words and values. In accepting others, you hold evaluation back and thereby learn more about the other. The holding back prevents many misperceptions. One powerful source of influence is your personal appeal or credibility. Credibility is in the eye of the beholder. Even the most competent, trustworthy person will have less credibility if he or she fails to listen and does not show acceptance of a speaker's ideas. You can also boost your credibility by showing that you are knowledgeable about all sides of an issue as a result of good listening. Table 3.1 presents some guidelines for good listening.

There are two major aspects of acceptance: accepting yourself and accepting others. When you can accept the different aspects of yourself, you can more readily accept others' feelings and motivations without judging them. Thus, acceptance is an important component of meaningful and productive relationships with others. Accepting others means understanding their points of view, knowing how and why they have such beliefs, and respecting them even if you do not agree with them. Thus, accepting is listening plus respect. Respect for others helps them express themselves openly without being afraid that they will be judged. Table 3.2 gives guidelines for listening for content, which involves listening with respect.

Table 3.1   Ten Keys to Effective Listening

Ten Keys to Effective Listening	The Bad Listener	The Good Listener
1. Find areas of interest.	Tunes out dry subjects.	Looks for benefits and opportunities; asks, "What's in it for me?"
2. Judge content, not delivery.	Tunes out if delivery is poor.	Judges content: skips over delivery errors.
3. Hold your fire.	Tends to enter into argument.	Doesn't judge until message is complete.
4. Listen for ideas.	Listens for facts.	Listens for central themes.
5. Be flexible.	Takes intensive notes using only one system.	Takes fewer notes; uses several different systems, depending on speaker.
6. Work at listening.	Shows no energy output. Attention is faked.	Works hard, exhibits active body state.
7. Resist distractions.	Distracted easily.	Fights or avoids distractions; tolerates bad habits; knows how to concentrate.
8. Exercise your mind.	Resists difficult, expository material; seeks light, recreational material.	Uses heavier material as exercise for the mind.
9. Keep your mind open.	Reacts to emotional words.	Interprets color words; does not get hung up on them.
10. Capitalize on the fact that *thought* is faster than *speech*.	Tends to daydream with slow speakers.	Challenges, anticipates, mentally summarizes; weighs the evidence; listens between the lines to tone of voice.

Source: Lyman Steil, Larry Barker, and Kittie Watson, *Effective Listening: Keys to Your Success* (Reading, Massachusetts: Addison-Wesley, 1983).

We usually assume that we understand another without bothering to check our assumptions. Paraphrasing and perception checking are skills that allow you to verify your understanding. When you paraphrase and check your perceptions, you not only clarify the meaning of the speaker's message, but you also communicate that what he or she said was important to you.

Table 3.2   Listening for Content

Ten Worst Listening Habits	Ten Best Listening Habits
Calling the subject "uninteresting."	Tuning in to see if there is anything you can use.
Criticizing the speaker's delivery, personal appearance, necktie, etc.	Getting the message, which is ten times as important as the speaker's appearance, etc.
Getting overstimulated and preparing a rebuttal.	Hearing the speaker out before you judge him or her.
Listening only for facts.	Listening for main ideas, principles, and concepts.
Trying to make an outline of everything you hear.	Listening two or three minutes before taking notes.
Faking attention to the speaker.	Not relaxing while listening; in good listening there is a collection of tensions inside.
Tolerating distractions in meeting.	Getting up and doing something about distractions—by shutting a window, closing a door, requesting the person to speak louder, etc.
Avoiding difficult material.	Learning to listen to difficult material.
Letting emotion-laden words affect you.	Identifying your own greatest word barriers.
Wasting the differential between speech speed (100 to 300 words per minute) and thought speed (cruising 800 words per minute).	a. Anticipating the next point to be made. b. Making contrast and comparison. c. Identifying the speaker's evidence. d. Practicing mental recapitulation.

Source: Adapted from Ralph G. Nichols and Leonard A. Stevens, *Are You Listening?* (New York: McGraw-Hill, 1957).

Active listening is listening to another without passing judgment on what is being said. It also implies feeding back what has been said to indicate that you understood what the person said and how he or she feels about it. It seems quite simple, but the implications of this orientation are tremendous. By withholding judgment and by showing that you understand the feelings of the other, you tell the person to be free to say more and that there is no risk of being judged and found stupid. In significant communication, you remove the threat that is always present. Effective communication is free to happen once that threat has been removed. By feeding back what the person says, you help build a positive work climate that is accepting, noncritical, and nonmoralizing. Feedback is examined in more detail later in this chapter.

Active listening indicates to the other person that he or she is fundamentally important and worth listening to, worth your attention, energy, and time. You cannot fake active listening, because paying attention is not enough. You must feel that other people are important in their own right and that by listening to them you are showing them respect.

Active listening is firmly based on the basic attitudes of the listener. You cannot use it as a technique if your fundamental attitudes about others are in conflict with its basic concepts. Unless you have a spirit that genuinely respects the potential worth of an individual and trusts that person's capacity for self-direction, you cannot begin to be an effective listener. Active listening is the greatest tool you can use in one-on-one communication. The power to listen is a remarkably sensitive skill. It is certainly the skill that makes managing truly effective and rewarding for all concerned. The ways you choose to listen influences others. How you listen may well determine how others listen to you.

Listening to Subordinates

Since most subordinates feel that management doesn't listen, it is important for managers to polish listening skills and thereby enhance their effectiveness.

The following guidelines will help.

1. Don't judge prematurely. Rather than judge, try to understand the message first.
2. Be opportunistic. You can find reasons to listen by asking yourself, "How can I use this information?"
3. Listen for feelings as well as ideas.
4. Try to identify main points and outline them in your mind. Look for the support given for the main points as well.
5. Ask questions and paraphrase. Questions seek new information, while paraphrasing reviews and ensures understanding.
6. Take occasional notes.
7. Repeat what you heard.

FEEDBACK

As active listening demonstrates, an integral part of reducing barriers in communication is making optimum use of feedback—both giving and receiving it. We continually adjust to the constant stream of messages we get from others during the course of a day. The number of messages you send or receive may vary, just as your ability to react appropriately may vary from one person to another. You can identify those who can give clear instructions, those who can do what they are asked, those who can understand complex information, and those who have difficultly in grasping new ideas.

Much of the ability to perform well in assignments is related to the ability to give and receive feedback. The effective communicator can pick up the cues offered by someone who does not understand instructions. The effective communicator can also predict what parts of a message are confusing, and restate or clarify those parts without being asked—simply because he or she senses the hearer's confusion.

The effectiveness of your communication is affected by the kinds of feedback you receive—whether negative or positive. We have a tendency to pretend we understand when we really do not to avoid looking stupid. As a result, we miss important messages and may give inappropriate feedback. Two guidelines are suggested: first, give more honest feedback about your understanding, and second, make it easy for the other to say that he or she does not understand. If you reduce the other's anxiety about asking questions by suggesting in advance that you may not be making your message clear, you receive more honest feedback.

Feedback is generally of two types: informing and reinforcing. Informing feedback helps the speaker adjust his or her message to ensure that it is understandable. Reinforcing feedback is usually evaluative, for example, telling the speaker what's liked and disliked about his or her message. Informing feedback comes in many forms. It may be a facial gesture, asking a question, or even answering a question. Informing feedback serves two important functions. It improves the accuracy of the message, and it puts the speaker at ease. In addition, it helps the speaker to feel more confident and the audience to form more accurate judgments about the speaker.

Reinforcing feedback can be either positive or negative. When we give positive reinforcement for good, right, or correct behavior, such feedback serves to change communication behavior in the desired direction and creates a favorable attitude in the recipient. Negative reinforcement for a behavior that was wrong or incorrect creates displeasure in the recipient, inhibits communication, and interferes with communication, creating frustration and avoidance.

When you give feedback, it is important that you avoid being defensive. To help the other feel accepted and respected, you need to create an atmosphere that is nondefensive. Following are guidelines for giving nondefensive feedback.

- Describe rather than evaluate.
- Be specific rather than general.
- Focus on sharing information rather than giving advice.
- Focus on the value the feedback may have for the recipient.
- Focus feedback in the here and now.
- Be direct .

Let's examine each of the guidelines.

Describe rather than evaluate.

Focus on behaviors rather than the person. "John, your accident report arrived after noon" is more constructive than "John, you're always late." To use description is to avoid evaluation of the other person or of his or her actions. Description attempts to remain neutral; judgment takes sides.

Be specific rather than general.

"Bill, I want you to improve your safety performance" is less constructive than "Bill, I want you to decrease accidents by 10 percent this month."

Focus on sharing information rather than giving advice.

Telling others what to do with the information you give does not leave them free to determine the appropriate course of action. Giving advice is a poor attempt at problem solving that does not give others leeway to make their own choices. Explore alternatives rather than provide solutions.

Focus on the value the feedback may have for the recipient rather than the relief it gives you.

If giving feedback is only making you feel good, you may not be helping as much as you are imposing. Be aware of how much feedback the person can handle at one time.

Focus feedback in the here and now rather than on something that occurred in the past.

To say to someone you are upset about something he or she did last week is unproductive; no one can change the past. Deal with the issue now, be it negative or positive.

Be direct rather than indirect.

Own your feelings and thoughts by saying, "I am mad at you," rather than, "You make me so mad."

MANAGERS' EXPECTATIONS: THE SELF-FULFILLING PROPHECY

You have a profound impact on the success or failure of each employee, whether you realize it or not. The difference between the top performer and the poor performer may be a result of how you treat them (Rosenthal, 1968). One of the most powerful influences on the performance of others is your own expectations. The best managers have confidence in themselves and in their ability to hire, develop, and motivate people, and largely because of that self-confidence, they communicate high expectations to others. You can increase or decrease an employee's initiative by using praise, feedback, or information. You can produce employees who perform well and feel good about themselves, or employees who perform poorly and feel bad about themselves.

Everybody has expectations of other people. We communicate those expectations with various cues. Employees tend to respond to these cues by adjusting their behavior to match the expectations. The result is that the original expectation becomes true. Let's say, for example, that you have just hired a new employee. You hired him because he meets the qualifications and received rave reviews from past employers. You feel confident that he will perform well and will need little direction. You suggest he attend all important meetings to keep informed and provide his insights. In those meetings you ask for his opinion, usually before those of other employees. You provide him with positive feedback and give him special projects. As a result of your positive expectations and the way you communicate them to the employee, the worker actually does perform extremely well. Expectations are natural and unavoidable. We form them in many ways, and many are preconceived. We prejudge either positively or negatively. We like to think we know what's going to happen before it happens, and we don't like to be proven wrong. We want to feel that we can control things. In our previous example, your preconceived expectations helped you to predict an employee's performance and made your job easier by eliminating the need to continually monitor his performance.

You cannot avoid communicating expectations because your messages are often nonverbal and unintentional. A nod of the head, prolonged eye contact, and tone of voice all communicate expectations. By soliciting an employee's opinions before those of other employees, sitting next to him, and listening to his ideas, you communicate positive expectations.

In a famous study of expectations, Robert Rosenthal (1968, p. 11) of Harvard University worked with elementary school children from eighteen classrooms. He randomly choose 20 percent of the children from each room and told the teachers they were "intellectual bloomers." He explained that these children could be expected to show remarkable gains during the year. At the end of the year the experimental children showed average intelligence-quotient gains of two points in verbal ability, seven points in reasoning, and four points in overall IQ. By what the teacher said, how and when she said it, her facial expression, posture, and touch, the teacher communicated to the children that she expected improved performance. The children changed their self-concept, their expectations of their own behavior, and their motivation.

Likewise, your employees behave according to the way you treat them. If you tell an employee that he's worthless, has no sense of right or wrong, and isn't going to amount to anything, he'll respond accordingly. If you tell him sincerely that he's important to you, that you have every confidence in his judgment, and that you're sure he's going to be successful in what he does, he'll respond accordingly. Wnen you transmit expectations to him, he reflects the image you've created for him.

Rosenthal (1868) documented this phenomenon in a number of case studies prepared during the past decade for major industrial concerns. These studies reveal that:

- What a manager expects of subordinates and the way he or she treats them largely determine their performance and career progress.
- A unique characteristic of superior managers is their ability to create high performance expectations that subordinates fulfill.
- Less effective managers fail to develop such expectations, and as a consequence the productivity of their subordinates suffers.
- Subordinates, more often than not, appear to do what they believe they are expected to do (Livingston, 1969).

In a study of the early managerial success of 49 college graduates who were management-level employees of an operating company of AT&T, David Berlew and Douglas Hall (1966) of Massachusetts Institute of Technology examined the career progress of these managers over a five-year period. They discovered that the employees' relative success as measured by salary increases and the company's estimate of each man's performance and potential depended largely on the company's expectations of them.

When employees are treated by their managers as super performers, they try to live up to that image and do what they know super performers are expected to do. But when employees with poor productivity records are treated by their managers as not having any chance of success, this negative expectation also becomes a managerial self-fulfilling prophecy.

According to Livingston (1969), unsuccessful employees have a great deal of difficulty maintaining their self-image and self-esteem. In response to low managerial expectations, they typically attempt to prevent additional damage to their egos by avoiding situations that might lead to greater failure. Low expectations and damaged egos lead employees to behave in a manner that increases the probability of failure, thereby fulfilling their managers' expectations.

Berlew and Hall found that what AT&T initially expected of its 49 college graduates was the most critical factor in their subsequent performance and success. The researchers concluded that "the .72 correlation between how much a company expects of a person in his or her first year and how much he or she contributes during the next five years is too compelling to be ignored" (Berlew and Hall, 1966, p. 365).

Not only do we have expectations about others, we have expectations about ourselves. Successful business leaders and their subordinates were reviewed to determine what traits the leaders had in common. One of the strongest characteristics was a positive self-image. These managers were able to create high expectations, while weaker managers could not. If you have confidence in your ability to develop employees and stimulate them to high achieve peak levels of performance, you naturally expect more of them and treat them with the assurance that your expectations will be met. If you have doubts about your ability to stimulate employees, you naturally expect less of them and treat them with less confidence (Livingston, 1969).

Expectations are a powerful ally of communication. Of all factors correlated with job satisfaction and performance, over 50 studies correlated high performance with expectations. We know that the best organizational performers can see the relationship between their performance and rewards. They can see the goals more clearly than others. The best performers are governed by expectations, not job satisfaction.

How Managers Communicate Negative Expectations

The following list tells how to set up negative expectations in employees.

- Seat low-expectation employees in less prestigious office areas away from the manager.
- Pay less attention to low-expectation employees in business situations. Smile at them less often and maintain less eye contact. Don't give them information about what's going on in the department.
- Call on low-expectation employees less often to work on special projects, state their opinions, or give presentations.

- Give low-expectation employees less time to state their opinions.
- Don't stay with low-expectation employees in failure situations (i.e., provide less help or give less advice to subordinates who really need it).
- Criticize low-expectation employees more frequently than others for making mistakes.
- Praise low-expectation employees more frequently than others for marginal or inadequate efforts.
- Praise low-expectation employees less frequently than others after successful efforts.
- Provide low-expectation employees with less-accurate and less-detailed feedback on job performance than high-expectation workers.
- Don't provide low-expectation employees with feedback about their job performance as often as others.
- Demand less work and effort from low-expectation employees than from high-expectation employees.
- Interrupt low-expectation employees more frequently than high-expectation employees.

EMPLOYEE NEEDS

In addition to managerial expectations, we need to consider the specific needs that employees seek to satisfy through their work. The list of specific work-related needs or motives that psychologists have identified is almost endless. Several basic groups of needs have been consistently cited in organizational behavior research as important to employees in jobs at various levels within organizations.

There are a number of motives, and they differ in how easily they can be adapted to different circumstances. They also differ in the degree to which they are influenced by heredity and environment. For example, intelligence remains rather constant throughout adult life, whereas achievement needs or managerial skills can be changed through learning experiences.

Perhaps one of the most frequently investigated work-related motives is achievement. Atkinson and McClelland (1966) define the motive as a desire to accomplish objectives and to experience the feeling of pride in the satisfaction derived from accomplishment. The need for achievement varies among individuals. High-need achievers tend to behave in characteristic fashion, according to McClelland. They tend to avoid both high and low risk, preferring tasks that involve a moderate amount of risk. High-need achievers do not like gambling. They also prefer immediate feedback on how well they are performing. They prefer jobs that have clear task definition and highly measurable and concrete results. They prefer to have money incentives associated with their work, and value money as a symbol of accomplishment rather than for the material goods it can buy. McClelland and his associates believe that the need for achievement is learned, and that where it is prevalent, business development will flourish.

GIVING CLEAR INSTRUCTIONS

Employees need to know why their job or a certain task is important and they need to know how it fits into the organization as a whole. They'll be able to perform better when they receive precise instructions. Give instructions in clear, simple terms. Prepare the other by explaining what you will be talking about. After giving instructions, be sure to summarize. We remember what we hear due to repetition.

It is important to begin at the employee's level. Start with what the employee already knows before proceeding to new information. Be specific. State what it is you want, when you want it, from whom, how you want it done, and what the end state should look like. For example, a manager might state, "Bob, I want you to get three estimates for our new safety posters. Please contact three vendors and have them submit a bid on our standard proposal form. Then, by Friday's status meeting, put together a one-page report recommending one of the vendors for the job." Give the employee time to ask questions. Be willing to take the time necessary to answer all questions and provide all the information the employee needs to accomplish the task. You may want to have the employee rephrase what you said to ensure accuracy.

In defining roles and giving instructions, it is easy to fall into a number of traps that prevent your message from getting across and instructions from being fulfilled. Following are some traps to guard against and tips for preventing them.

Inflexibility

There are as many ways to express a thought as there are people in this world. Flexibility in communicating an idea or thought requires that you tailor your message to the person you are talking to. Employees change in attitude, from day to day, and according to different situations. It is to your advantage to assess the situation prior to uttering an idea in order to tailor your message to the employee.

Language Cosmetics

To create an impression, we often dress up our words. When we make our words look better, we are also being less specific and more abstract, creating a tendency to mislead the other. For example, we refer to poverty as "low income," firing as being "selected out," unemployment as "employment development." We may use words to convey the impression that a problem is solved or a task is completed when such is not the case. "I'm in the process of analyzing or researching," is an example. "We are assigning major priority to the early completion of the preliminary stages of the program," means "With any luck we can forget the matter completely." Be aware of cosmetic language, and say things as they really are.

Unclear Roles

In order for an employee to perform a task, three variables must be present. First, the employee must have the necessary skills and abilities to do the job. Second, the employee must be motivated. Finally, the employee needs to know what is expected; in other words, the person must have an accurate perception of his or her role in the task accomplishment. You can assist by making sure the employee clearly understands that role and what is expected.

Pseudo Decision Making

Managers often try to involve employees in decisions about how a task is to be completed under the rationale that if they use employee input, employees are more likely to support and follow through with the task. Many managers fall into the trap of pseudoparticipative decision making. They may engage employees, but if the employees' ideas are not valued or accepted, the process has lost its value. Participative decision making needs to take place on a daily basis rather than once a month or twice a year. It requires constant validation, in which employees identify and accept decisions on a daily basis. If you don't actually want to involve the employee, don't invite him or her to participate.

HOW CAN YOU PUT COMMUNICATION TO WORK?

You can influence the success of your subordinates by doing the following:

- Create a climate of acceptance.
- Smile.
- Nod your head approvingly.

- Use prolonged eye contact.
- Be supportive, friendly, accepting, and encouraging.
- Assign tasks and projects with confidence.
- Make assignments challenging and recognize achievement.
- Encourage employee contribution.
- Seek out opinions that disagree with yours.
- Give assistance or encouragement in solving problems only when absolutely necessary.
- Praise good work.
- Don't criticize mistakes; express confidence that next time the work will be right.

By communicating precisely what is expected in performance and how to achieve the desired results and providing positive feedback for the desired performance, you help create motivated employees who feel good about themselves. The results of unclear expectations, on the other hand, are employee frustration, failure, unhealthy competition, and fear of risk taking.

4
Interpersonal Influence ▲

INTERPERSONAL INFLUENCE AND TRUST

The amount of cooperation you get from people depends on whether or not trust exists in your working relationship. As a manager you are faced with the decision whether to trust without knowing if it's safe to build a trusting relationship. In choosing to trust, you may be seen as warm, compassionate, and sincere or as gullible and stupid. If you choose not to trust you may be seen as hard-nosed and shrewd or as distant and untrustworthy. Do you buy the sob stories some employees give you to get out of work and run the risk of being seen as a weak manager, or do you act like a hard-nosed supervisor who is not easily conned? In either case, your behavior will affect that of your employees.

According to Rossiter and Pearce (1975), trust exists when a relationship is characterized by some degree of vulnerability and predictability and by alternative options. Vulnerability suggests that the outcomes of the other's actions significantly affect you. If somebody has no effect on you, there is no need for you to trust that person. Predictability refers to the degree of confidence you have in your guess as to what the other person will do. When predictability is low, you cannot have much confidence that the other person will behave in a certain way. You may have hope, but not trust. Having alternative options implies that you are free to do something else besides trust. Trust is present only by choice. If any one of these three characteristics is missing, trust is missing as well. If what happens to you depends on the other's behavior, if you have some basis for predicting how the other will behave, and if you have a choice about your own behavior, then you are in a situation in which trust is an option. This is usually the case in a manager-subordinate relationship.

To trust is risky, because you increase your vulnerability to the other. Trust means you will allow another to affect you. To do so you must believe that the other is both willing and able to behave in ways that will not hurt you. Note that abilities are crucial. Is the other able or competent to perform the action you predict will take place? There is no sure way to get others to trust you. While trusting others sometimes encourages them to trust you, distrusting others almost always promotes distrust. Trust is built through risks mutually taken one by one in a given relationship. To establish a trusting relationship requires that you begin trusting even though you are not sure that the other will prove to be trustworthy. You develop trust through incremental steps.

Nor can you force trust on another. Therefore, you must decide whether the risks are worth taking and whether you can afford to take them. This implies that to have others trust you, you must actively take some initiative and not simply wait for others to make the first move. If you want to be trusted, you have to make the first gesture, which always involves some risk.

According to Myers and Myers (1985), developing trust in others is not simple. It depends on both your behavior and the ability of the other to trust and take risks. You have little control over another's ability to take risks; you do, however, have some control over the degree of risk involved for the other. If the messages you send are reliable, if most of the time you come through on your word, if your actions match your words and your nonverbal messages fit your verbal ones, others can develop the ability to predict your actions and thus minimize their chances of guessing wrong about what you will do.

You also have some degree of control over the outcome of risk-taking behavior. The way you respond to employees who take risks and make mistakes affects their decision to take risks again.

You may tell an employee to go ahead with a project on his or her own and that you will support whatever he or she comes up with. If you reprimand the employee when the product is not exactly as you would have wished, you make it unlikely that the employee will believe that you meant what you said.

Trust is a self-fulfilling prophecy. If you are taught to trust, unless given a reason not to, you will act more open, use less strategy, and be less defensive. If you are taught not to trust unless it's proven that you should, you will be closed and defensive. Each attitude is a self-fulfilling prophecy because it becomes a reality. When you act and really are trustworthy, others will tend to do the same. You must trust yourself in order to trust others.

Figure 4.1 will help you assess the trust in your relationships.

Figure 4.1   Developing Trust: A Behavioral Assessment

Assess your relationships by answering the following questions with Frequently (F), Sometimes (S), or Never (N).

		F	S	N
1.	I share personal facts with my subordinates.	___	___	___
2.	I am open to subordinates' ideas and am willing to use them, even if it means forgoing my own ideas.	___	___	___
3.	I stand behind my subordinates and support them by giving them what they need.	___	___	___
4.	I allow my subordinates to get involved in decision making.	___	___	___
5.	I value my subordinates and communicate that to them.	___	___	___
6.	I am aware of my subordinates' needs.	___	___	___
7.	I speak with my subordinates daily.	___	___	___
8.	I am frank with my subordinates.	___	___	___
9.	I understand my own strengths and weaknesses.	___	___	___
10.	I allow my subordinates to take risks and try out their own ideas.	___	___	___
11.	When mistakes occur, I focus on solving the problem and prevention in the future rather than on blaming the person who caused it.	___	___	___

DIMENSIONS OF A TRUSTING RELATIONSHIP

By exhibiting trusting behavior, you not only improve relationships and communication, you also improve the way others respond to you. If you are perceived as trustworthy, others will also perceive you as more credible, and as a result, they will trust you more. When you exhibit trusting behaviors, you fit the descriptions that follow.

You are **aware** when your outward behavior reflects your inner feelings and thoughts, when you explicitly recognize how your feelings are influencing your behavior, when you recognize and respond to the feelings you experience. Your awareness may be indicated by a statement such as, "I feel somewhat at a loss, since we don't have a topic," instead of "We seem to be floundering around without something we can get our teeth into," or, "I'm not sure I want to say how I feel about you," instead of "I don't think we should get personal."

You are **self-accepting** when you are able to accept your own feelings without denying them, giving rationalizations for them, or apologizing for them. Self-acceptance may be evidenced by a statement such as, "I'm bored with what you are saying," instead of "This is a boring topic," or "I'm angry at myself for being ineffective," instead of "This group is not getting anywhere."

You are **accepting of others** when you are able to accept the feelings and thoughts of others without trying to change them, when you are able to let others be themselves even though they are different from you. Acceptance of others may be shown by listening in order to understand and without trying to refute, by trying not to argue, by asking questions in order to understand, and by not judging another.

You are **supportive** when you seek ways to help others reach goals that are important to them, try to understand what others want to do although you may not agree with their conclusions, or encourage others to try behavior that is new to them. Support may be seen in comments such as, "Could you tell me how I might help you reach our objective?" or, "I am not sure I agree with what you are proposing, but I support your effort to get something going," or, "Let me see if I understand what you want us to do."

You are **risk-taking** when you go "beyond the known" by experimenting with new behavior, when you want to accomplish something or support someone else more than you want to play it safe or keep your cool, and when you are willing to risk being angry, anxious, caring, driving, or retreating even though these behaviors may make you appear emotional, inept, or unintelligent or may arouse your anxiety. Risk taking may be shown by initiating feedback on your behavior, by supporting someone when it is not clear what the consequences will be, or by giving feedback to others on their behavior.

You are **problem-centered** when you focus on problems facing a group rather than on control or method and when you try to learn by solving problems yourself rather than using someone else's solutions. Problem centering may be seen in your efforts to find out what is blocking a group, to increase personal effectiveness, and to probe beyond the symptoms. Problem centering assumes that more work gets done when individuals and groups learn how to solve problems than when they maintain established patterns of method, control, leadership, or feedback.

You are **leveling** when you are able to be open about your feelings and thoughts, when your outward behavior reflects your inner experience.

POWER IN RELATIONSHIPS

The trust that others accord you is a dynamic source of power, which we have defined as interpersonal power. Interpersonal power is not something you possess; rather, it is something others give to you. In other words, you are powerless without others. They trust you and award you power. Interpersonal power gives you the potential to influence others. Interpersonal power carries a tremendous amount of responsibility. You keep your power by restraining its use and by using it wisely for the personal development of others. Such power will be instantly lost if misused. One does not have the option of not using power, but one does have the options of productive use or destructive use of power. Relationships have a better chance of working in the long term if there is equity in the power involved. Unrestrained use of power usually comes back to damage the one who uses it. Effective use of power involves restraint in its use.

CALIBRATED DISCLOSURE

Disclosure is making something known, revealing it, and calibrated disclosure is the act of gradually making yourself known to another. Every time you interact, you reveal something about yourself. Consciously choosing to disclose something about yourself only constitutes about 2 percent of your total communication but it is the most important part.

In the business environment we tend to disclose little about ourselves. We avoid disclosure because we fear being evaluated negatively, losing control of another, hurting the other, projecting a negative image, and revealing information that might be used against us at some future time. Disclosure may be viewed as an act of weakness, exhibitionism, or even mental illness. At the same time, disclosure can be used to increase trust and foster open communication and an open working climate. In such pursuits, the manager plays a key role. You can use calibrated disclosure to create a supportive climate and open communication and to encourage disclosure from employees. The amount of disclosure that occurs in any business relationship is an indicator of the health of the relationship and the work climate.

Calibrated disclosure is not a goal in itself but a means of establishing and enhancing relationships. The issues of what we should say about ourselves, to whom we should say it, and how we should express ourselves are difficult to resolve. In fact there is little research to determine what the optimal degree of disclosure should be. Social norms govern the appropriateness of disclosure. Violating these norms by disclosing too much too soon may well have a negative impact. For this reason, it is possible to disagree strongly with the position that total openness is a necessary characteristic of effective relationships.

On the other hand, although some people have an inappropriately high rate and level of disclosure (telling us more than we'd like to hear), for most of us the problem is a different one. Often we do not reveal enough of ourselves even when disclosure is appropriate and legitimate. Some people remain relatively private because they fear the consequences of disclosure. Others just don't know how to reveal themselves to others.

Although the amount of disclosure varies from one person to another, almost everyone shares important information about himself at one time or another. Following are several reasons for disclosure.

- Catharsis: Sometimes we disclose information to get it off our chests.
- Self-clarification: Sometimes you can clarify your beliefs, opinions, thoughts, attitudes, and feelings by talking about them with another person.
- Self-validation: If you disclose information with the hope of seeking the listener's agreement, you are seeking validation of a belief you hold about yourself. On a deeper level, this sort of validating disclosure seeks confirmation of important parts of your self-concept.
- Reciprocity: Research indicates that disclosing information about yourself encourages another person to begin sharing.
- Impression formation: You may choose to disclose to create a particular impression of yourself.
- Relationship maintenance: Relationships need disclosure to stay healthy and develop. Without disclosure interaction becomes limited and shallow.

We can become intimidated by the concept of disclosure, believing that it refers to the revelation of our intimate thoughts and feelings. While this type of total openness may be appropriate in certain relationships at certain times, there are other less intimate levels of disclosure equally valuable to relational growth. Whatever its context, disclosing information reveals that which would otherwise be inaccessible to a listener. This information may take many forms; basic personal data, preferences, beliefs, and values are all legitimate forms of disclosure. You can also disclose what you sense, think, feel, want, intend, and do.

Calibrated disclosure, appropriately done, can be helpful to your communication. The payoffs include (1) improving accuracy of communication and adding thoughts and feelings to the already public material you share with others, (2) getting to know more about another, and (3) getting to know more about yourself. Calibrated disclosure is an important element in developing relationships with others and in knowing yourself (Myers and Myers, 1985). However, you must be sensitive to your needs as well as the needs of others. When you are able to disclose in a sensitive manner, you have made progress in developing predictability about how you and others will act in a wide variety of situations.

Calibrated disclosure is characterized by the presentation of information that is personal as well as purposely and honestly communicated. The information must be unavailable or difficult to get except from the person disclosing. The final qualification for an act of calibrated disclosure can be defined only from the sender's viewpoint; what is personal information for one sender may be only surface information for a receiver or another sender.

Disclosure is not always appropriate. There are certain situations when disclosing too much too fast or to the wrong persons may have negative consequences for you. Be sensitive to each situation to determine if it is appropriate to disclose. Use the following guidelines in determining when disclosure is appropriate. According to Myers and Myers (1985, p. 77), you may want to disclose in the following situations:

1. In an ongoing relationship where disclosing is not an isolated incident.
2. When you think the other is likely to disclose also.
3. When the disclosure is relevant to the present situation.
4. When disclosure is about positive rather than negative things. Very often the person who discloses too much negative information about himself or herself is considered poorly adjusted.
5. When the disclosure helps to improve the relationship.
6. When you are sensitive to what effects the disclosure will have on the other.
7. When disclosure is gradual.
8. When you trust the other and are sure the other trusts you.

Using calibrated disclosure improves working relationships; serves as a reality check for thoughts, feelings, and perceptions; and promotes organizational health. Concealing yourself from others takes a great deal of energy and creates a great deal of stress. The energy drain can lead to loneliness, depression, and physical and mental illness. When struggling to actively avoid becoming known by others, you cannot be yourself. Using disclosure releases stress, expands self-knowledge, and increases satisfaction with relationships. How willing are you to be open with others? Figure 4.2, a survey of disclosure behavior, can help you find out.

Figure 4.2   Calibrated Disclosure Survey

Complete this survey to help you assess your understanding of your disclosure behavior in relationships. There are no right or wrong answers. The best answer is the one that comes closest to representing your efforts toward good working relationships. In each statement, the first sentence gives a situation and the second sentence gives a reaction. For each statement, indicate the number that is closest to the way you would handle the situation, using the following key:

> 5 = You *always* would act this way.
> 4 = You *frequently* would act this way.
> 3 = You *sometimes* would act this way.
> 2 = You *seldom* would act this way.
> 1 = You *never* would act this way.

Try to relate each question to your own personal experience. Take as much time as you need to give a true and accurate answer for yourself.

1. A coworker's mannerisms and habits are getting on your nerves and irritating you. More and more you avoid interaction.

   Never   1   2   3   4   5   Always

2. In a moment of weakness, you make public the secret of a coworker, who later finds out and confronts you about it. You admit to it and discuss how to handle this better in the future.

   Never   1   2   3   4   5   Always

3. You have a boss who never seems to have time for you. You ask him about it and tell him how you feel.

   Never   1   2   3   4   5   Always

4. Your secretary is upset at you because you have inconvenienced her, and she tells you how she feels. You tell her she is too sensitive and is overreacting.

   Never   1   2   3   4   5   Always

5. You had a disagreement with a coworker, and now he ignores you whenever he's around. You decide to ignore him back.

   Never   1   2   3   4   5   Always

6. An employee has pointed out that you never seem to have time for him. You explain why you have been busy and try for mutual understanding.

    Never   1   2   3   4   5   Always

7. At great inconvenience, you arrange to take an employee to a doctor's office. When you arrive to take her to the appointment, you find she has decided not to go. You explain to her how you feel and try to reach an understanding about future favors.

    Never   1   2   3   4   5   Always

8. You have argued with a coworker and are angry with him, and you ignore him when you meet. He tells you how he feels and asks about restoring the relationship. You ignore him and walk away.

    Never   1   2   3   4   5   Always

9. You know a secret about upcoming cutbacks that you have told only to your closest associate. The next day, another coworker asks you about the cutbacks. You deny that you know anything and decide never to share any privileged information with your associate from now on.

    Never   1   2   3   4   5   Always

10. A coworker tells you about some of your mannerisms and habits that get on his nerves. You discuss these and look at some possible ways of dealing with the problem.

    Never   1   2   3   4   5   Always

11. A personal friend gets involved in a cover-up that you believe will lead the company into serious trouble. You decide to tell him that you disapprove of his involvement in the cover-up.

    Never   1   2   3   4   5   Always

12. In a moment of weakness you make public the secret of a coworker, who finds out and confronts you about it. You deny it firmly.

    Never   1   2   3   4   5   Always

13. You have a boss who never seems to have time for you. You decide to forget it and to start looking for a new job.

    Never   1   2   3   4   5   Always

14. You are involved in a cover-up and a personal friend tells you of his disapproval and fear that you will get in serious trouble. You tell your friend to mind his own business.

    Never   1   2   3   4   5   Always

15. A coworker's mannerisms and habits are getting on your nerves and irritating you. You explain your feelings and look for a mutual solution to the problem.

    Never   1   2   3   4   5   Always

16. An employee has pointed out that you never seem to have time for him. You walk away.

Never   1   2   3   4   5   Always

17. Your personal friend gets involved in a cover-up that you believe will lead the company into serious trouble. You decide to mind your own business.

Never   1   2   3   4   5   Always

18. Your secretary is upset because you have inconvenienced her. She tells you how she feels. You try to understand and agree on a way to keep it from happening again.

Never   1   2   3   4   5   Always

19. You had a disagreement with a coworker, and now he ignores you whenever he is around. You tell him how his actions make you feel and ask about restoring your relationship.

Never   1   2   3   4   5   Always

20. A coworker tells you about some of your mannerisms and habits that get on his nerves. You listen and walk away.

Never   1   2   3   4   5   Always

21. At great inconvenience, you arrange to take an employee to the doctor's office. When you arrive to take her to the appointment, you find that she has decided not to go. You say nothing but resolve never to do any favors for that person again.

Never   1   2   3   4   5   Always

22. You have argued with a coworker and are angry, and you ignore him when you meet. He tells you how he feels and asks about restoring the relationship. You discuss ways of maintaining your relationship even though you disagree.

Never   1   2   3   4   5   Always

23. You have privileged information about upcoming cutbacks that you have told only your closest associate. The next day, a coworker asks you about the cutbacks. You call your associate and ask him about it, trying to come to an understanding of how to handle these situations better in the future.

Never   1   2   3   4   5   Always

24. You are involved in a cover-up, and your personal friend tells you of his disapproval and fear that the company will get in serious trouble. You tell your friend to mind his own business.

Never   1   2   3   4   5   Always

Scoring

In this survey, there are twelve questions that deal with your willingness to self-disclose and twelve questions that are concerned with your receptivity to feedback. Transfer your scores to this answer key. Reverse the scoring for all questions that are starred; that is, if you answered 5, record a 1; if you answered 4, record a 2; if you answered 3, record a 3. Then add the scores in each column.

Willingness to Disclose	Receptivity to Feedback
1. * _____	2. _____
3. _____	4. _____
5. * _____	6. _____
7. _____	8. * _____
9. * _____	10. _____
11. _____	12. * _____
13. * _____	14. _____
15. _____	16. * _____
17. * _____	18. _____
19. _____	20. * _____
21. * _____	22. _____
23. _____	24. * _____
TOTAL _____	TOTAL _____

On the summary sheet, add the totals for receptivity to feedback and willingness to self-disclose to arrive at an index of interpersonal risk taking.

Summary Sheet

	Your score
Receptivity to Feedback	_____
Willingness to Self-Disclose	_____
Interpersonal Risk Taking	_____

Plot your scores on the axes below. Draw horizontal and vertical lines from those points.

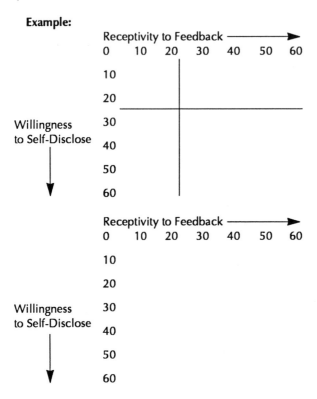

Example:

Figure 4.3   **The Johari Window: Interpreting the Results of Calibrated Disclosure**

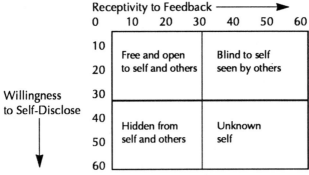

Source: Adapted from Joseph Luft and Harry Ingham, *Of Hman Interaction* (Palo Alto, CA: National Press Books, 1969).

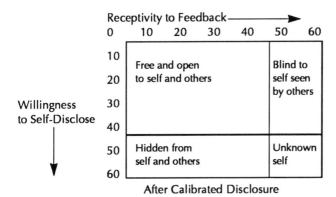

After Calibrated Disclosure

Note: Source unknown.

As Figure 4.3 illustrates, using calibrated disclosure results in more understanding of yourself, both by yourself and by others. In addition, the more trusting you are of others in opening your window, the more trusting they will be of you (Luft and Ingham, 1969).

OTHER MOTIVATING TECHNIQUES

Productivity is correlated with the variables presented below. When you issue job instructions, consider these factors.

- The amount of confidence and trust between the supervisor and the employee
- The degree of the supervisor's interest in the subordinate
- The supervisor's understanding of employee problems
- The amount of company-sponsored training and assistance
- The availability to employees of tools to do the job
- The supervisor's approachability
- The frequency and appropriateness of employee recognition by the supervisor
- The degree of adequate information given by the supervisor about the employee's performance
- The degree of open expression of ideas and opinions from employees
- Employee control over method of task accomplishment

Many managers say they know these elements and think they provide them. Their assumptions may be wrong. Rensis Likert (1976) compared the responses of supervisors and subordinates by asking supervisors, "How do you give recognition for good work done by employees in your work group?" and asking employees, "How does your supervisor give recognition for good work done by employees in your work group?" Table 4.1 gives the frequencies with which supervisors and employees responded "very often."

Table 4.1   Attitude Comparison:
            Recognition for Good Work

	Rate at which Supervisors Responded "Very Often"	Rate at which Employees Responded "Very Often"
Provides privileges	52%	14%
Provides more responsibility	48%	10%
Provides positive feedback	82%	13%
Provides sincere praise	80%	14%
Provides training	64%	9%
Provides more interesting work	51%	5%

Source: Adapted from Rensis Likert, *New Patterns of Management* (New York, McGraw-Hill, 1976).

What Really Motivates Your Employees?

There are certain variables that promote employee job satisfaction and certain variables that promote employee motivation. Herzberg (1959) has identified these variables and asserts that we can make a dissatisfied worker satisfied, although this does not necessarily mean that the worker will be motivated. You can improve employee motivation by using the factors that motivate rather than satisfy.

Determinants of employee satisfaction include the following:
- Money
- Status
- Relationship with supervisor
- Company policies
- Work rules
- Working conditions

Determinants of employee motivation are as follows:
- Sense of achievement
- Recognition
- Enjoyment of the job
- Possibility for advancement
- Responsibility
- Chance for growth

Know How Your Employees Respond

The key to understanding motivation lies in the awareness of how a reward is experienced by the employee receiving it. Some rewards can actually damage job performance by squelching interest and motivation. Some rewards are extrinsic and some are intrinsic. Extrinsic rewards include money, title, office location, and parking location, to name a few. Intrinsic rewards include recognition, responsibility, achievement, and opportunities for personal growth, which might necessitate time off.

Employees who see themselves as working solely for money or approval find their jobs less pleasurable. They focus narrowly on the task at hand, do it as quickly as possible, and take few risks. If an employee feels that the task is something he or she has to get through to get the prize, less creativity is used.

Employees need to be motivated from within. If not, after the cash bonus is received, for example, the motivation is gone. Employees are motivated because of accomplishment. Your responsibility is not to motivate employees (motivation is not something you do to another); it is to establish an environment in which your employees can be self-motivated. This means helping them to accomplish worthwhile work *and* acknowledging them when they accomplish something important and worthwhile.

MOTIVATION: A VALUE-FOR-VALUE EXCHANGE

Motivation is also influenced by how an employee perceives he or she is being treated in comparison to other employees. Most employees make a contribution to an organization for which they expect certain outcomes or rewards. By communicating and comparing rewards with other employees, employees gather information to determine whether the effort-reward exchange has been to their advantage. When an employee's efforts are relatively equal in relation to the earned rewards in comparison to others, he or she is likely to be satisfied. It is perceived fairness that stimulates behavior and satisfaction.

A major determinant not only of satisfaction but also of job effort and performance is the degree of balance an employee perceives between his or her efforts and the rewards received from performing a task. When dissatisfaction occurs, the employee will attempt to reduce the inequity through various means. An employee will feel inequity when he or she is underpaid or overpaid and when effort is high and pay is low while another's effort and pay are high (Adams, 1963). To reduce dissatisfaction the employee may behave as follows:

- Increase or decrease effort
- Devalue the job or reward

- Quit
- Take longer breaks and/or work fewer hours
- Convince others to produce less
- Pilfer company supplies for personal use
- Compare his job and pay with those of other workers

(Adams, 1963, pp. 422–436)

MOTIVATING THROUGH POSITIVE REINFORCEMENT

We can use the basics of reinforcement theory to pinpoint how reinforcement can increase or decrease an employee's behavior. In essence, the theory states that using positive reinforcement will increase the probability of the behavior you desire from your employee. The theory compares the results of using positive and negative reinforcement in addition to punishment and extinction (Skinner, 1969). Let's explore how these techniques can improve employee performance.

Positive Reinforcement

Let's say, for instance, that one of your employees has completed a major project that will reduce exposure to accidents. You give that employee positive feedback at your next staff meeting. By doing so, you have created a pleasant experience for the employee and also let other staff members know what you want from employees. As a result, that employee and possibly others will try to do something to achieve such recognition at the next staff meeting.

We pursue experiences that are pleasant to us, so positive reinforcement is an excellent motivational technique. Through positive means, not only do you get the performance you desire, but you also help people to reach their fullest potential, which improves morale.

Negative Reinforcement

Perhaps you have noticed employees leaving work early. You believe it is only fair for employees to put in a full day's work, so you remind the employees of standard work hours. Later you hear word that the employees are taking fifteen more minutes at lunch. So you send out a memo to remind employees of standard lunch hours and break times. When you use negative feedback, surprisingly enough, employees will continue the behavior.

Punishment

Let's say, for example, that one of your employees made a mistake and had an accident. You are upset, and during the staff meeting you yell at the employee. Using such punishment will make the employee feel a good deal of anxiety. When you use punishment, all employees will seek to avoid future punishments by such behavior as hiding accidents. Punishment is an unreliable type of reinforcement (Skinner, 1969).

Extinction

Providing no reinforcement at all can help to stop unwanted behaviors. When an act gets no reinforcement (positive or negative), it usually disappears.

When to Use Reinforcement

You can give reinforcement in a number of ways. First, you can give it according to a particular time frame, as in yearly performance appraisals. Many managers give employees bonuses at Christmas. If you only issue reinforcement according to a particular time frame, employees may work very hard prior to the bonus or appraisal and slack off the rest of the year.

Second, you can give reinforcement after employees reach a certain quota. Many managers give raises for meeting a sales quota and find that employees produce only what is required and little more.

Finally, you can vary the reinforcement so that the employee never knows when to expect it. Employees might keep performing well because they never know when a reward or evaluation is forthcoming. If your superior tells you he or she will be visiting your division next week but is not sure which day it will be, your department might operate at top performance for the duration of that week. Many organizations use similar techniques, among them unannounced inspections or behavior sampling, to monitor employee performance and to keep employees performing as desired.

Using Rewards

Potentially the single most useful reward that you have at hand is praise. While there is always enough to go around, you should be careful not to give it for the wrong reasons. Managers can and do reward the wrong behaviors unknowingly (Kerr, 1977). Often we reward the very behavior we try to discourage, and the desired behavior is not rewarded. When focusing on equity and objectivity, we seldom reward for team building, good interpersonal relationships, or creativity. Organizational reward systems can do the same. Universities reward research and not teaching, so teachers turn their efforts to research. Enforcing rigid compliance to work hours and breaks rewards punctuality rather than job performance.

Not everyone likes or needs the same things, but each of us knows how we would like to be recognized, what we would like to get. If you want to use rewards effectively, tune in to your people, understand their needs, and give them what they need.

Performance = Skills and Abilities + Clear Expectations + Motivation

Provided your employee has these three components, he or she will perform. Regardless of what the performance entails, if the person has all the required skills and abilities, receives clear and positive expectations from management, and is motivated, any task can and will be performed.

To conclude the chapter, try exploring your employees' view of you, using Figure 4.4.

Figure 4.4   Motivational Checklist for Managers

How do your employees see you? Ask yourself the following questions and circle your response.

1. Do you:
   a. try to help your employees understand company objectives and how they contribute to them?
   b. let your employees try to figure out for themselves how company objectives apply to them?
2. Do you:
   a. try to give your employees all the information they want?
   b. give your employees only as much information as they need?
3. Do you:
   a. expect superior performance and give credit for a job well done?
   b. expect employees to do an adequate job and only comment when something goes wrong?
4. Do you:
   a. have consistently high expectations of your employees?
   b. change your expectations of employees from day to day?
5. Do you:
   a. try to see the merit in employees' ideas even if they differ from yours?
   b. believe your ideas are the best because you're the boss?
6. Do you:
   a. encourage employees to reach out in new directions?
   b. try to protect them from taking big risks?

7. Do you:
   a. try to correct mistakes and determine how they can be prevented in the future?
   b. try to find out who caused the problem when something goes wrong?
8. Do you:
   a. try to be easy to talk to even when under pressure?
   b. send signals suggesting that employees have to pick carefully the best time to speak with you?
9. Do you:
   a. take employee mistakes in stride, as long as those involved can learn from them?
   b. allow little room for mistakes, especially those that might embarrass you?

If you chose answer "B" to all of the above, you are probably already providing a highly motivated climate for your employees.

Source: Adapted from M. Scott Meyers, "Conditions for Manager Motivation," *Harvard Business Review*, January/February 1966.

5
One-to-One Communication ▲

THE IMPORTANCE OF ONE-TO-ONE COMMUNICATION

In the late 1980s, management theory generally and safety management particularly emphasized one-to-one communication as the primary mode of communication between management and the worker. Perhaps the trend started with Situational Management of the One-Minute Manager (Blanchard and Johnson, 1982) concepts. At any rate, the change has taken place—today we perceive that the communication process should take place mostly on a one-to-one basis instead of by memo or in staff meetings.

One-to-one communication, a form of interpersonal communication, is the most common form of exchange. Consider the following examples: Tom, a safety manager, is developing a proposal for a new safety program. He needs some specific information on accident rates, so he walks down the hall to John and asks some questions. Tom also conducts performance appraisals as well as goal-setting and problem-solving sessions with each employee on a regular basis.

Interpersonal communication happens all the time. In a typical organization, such communication takes many different forms, including employment interviews, counseling, sales pitches, performance appraisals, goal-setting sessions, new employee orientations, complaint handling, and exit interviews. Interpersonal communication can be structured and formal, as in interviews, or unstructured and less formal, as in casual conversations. The difference between a conversation and an interview is that interviewing has a specific purpose, where conversations may or may not be directed toward a given result.

Successful interpersonal communication begins before two parties face one another. Whether you are the boss or the subordinate, background work can make the difference between success and disappointment.

PLANNING FOR ONE-TO-ONE COMMUNICATION

Define your objectives ahead of time, whether you are planning to reprimand an employee, sell a product, or hire an employee. If you are selling a product, is your goal to get a single order or to build a long-term relationship with your client? In a grievance interview, is your goal to ask for specific changes or simply to have your concerns acknowledged? Make your goal as clear as possible. Consider, for instance, the following variation in goals:

Vague: Improve employee's behavior

Better: Train employee to handle recording of accidents

Best: Train employee to follow the new accident recording system

Analyze the Other's Point of View

Just as in giving a presentation, whether you are the initiator or the person being contacted, you have the best chance of success when you have analyzed the other person and developed a plan based on your analysis. Your analysis ought to cover the other's self-image, knowledge level, image of you, and attitude. To understand these factors, ask yourself the following questions:

- If I were the other person, how would I feel about the subject?
- What does the other person know about the topic of discussion?
- How does this person view me?
- What does this person say about the topic?
- What does this person's behavior reveal about the topic?

Prepare a List of Discussion Topics

Once you have identified your objective, you will need to identify specifics that should be addressed in the exchange. For example:

Objective: To have the boss view me as an ambitious, articulate person who knows about and can serve the company's needs.

List of Topics and Reminders

1. Discuss my short-term and long-term career goals.
2. Answer all questions completely and in an organized fashion.
3. Share my knowledge about the company's products and financial condition.

Determine the Best Format and Structure

Each type of one-to-one exchange calls for different levels of planning and produces different results. When structuring an exchange, keep in mind that you need to choose the best structure for the specific objective and for the person you are interacting with.

In a highly structured exhange you can get more accurate information and be more consistent; however, this kind of interaction also creates more stress for the participants. Highly structured exchanges may require precise wording or a specific order in which questions are asked (Pashaliah and Crissy, 1953). Highly structured exchanges are commonly used in market research, opinion polls, and attitude surveys. Such exchanges are easier to tabulate and therefore useful for surveying large numbers of respondents. Often in employment screening interviews this structure is used so that a number of interviewers can get the same questions answered without personal opinion affecting the final decision. The highly structured exchange can promote greater interrater reliability.

A less structured exchange usually consists of an agenda without specific questions. Such an exchange allows considerable flexibility with regard to questions and is more relaxing for the participants. In a relaxed setting, you are likely to get more accurate information and a greater amount of it than in one that is not relaxed. Figure 5.1 indicates some pros and cons of various degrees of structure in interpersonal exchanges.

Figure 5.1   Advantages and Disadvantages of Structured Interpersonal Communication

	Not Structured	Moderately Structured	Highly Structured
Amount of potential information	high		low
Amount of precision and reliability	low		high
Control over the situation	low		high
Communication skill required	high		low
Freedom to adapt to different situations	high		low
Amount of preparation required	low		high

━━ = high   —— = medium   – – = low

Knowing that some structure is beneficial and that you want the other person to be relaxed, you may find it advantageous to use a moderately structured exchange. In this case, you would prepare a list of topics to be covered, anticipate their probable order, and list several major questions and possible follow-up probes. This provides a flexible plan that you can use or adapt as circumstances warrant.

Consider Possible Questions

As you might expect, the type and quality of questions are the biggest factors in determining the success of any exchange. There are several factors you might consider when planning questions.

Open versus Closed Questions

Closed questions restrict the other's response and allow you to get a single-answer response. Examples of closed questions include:

- How long have your worked there?
- When will the report be ready?
- Do you think you can do the job?
- Would you be willing to transfer?

Many closed questions call for a "yes" or "no" response. Open questions invite broader, more detailed responses. Examples of open questions include:

- Tell me about yourself.
- Tell me about your experience around here.
- What would you do if you were in my position?

See Figure 5.2 for the benefits and disadvantages of different kinds of questions.

Figure 5.2   Advantages and Disadvantages of Open versus Closed Questions

	Highly Open	Moderately Open	Highly Closed
Amount of potential information	high		low
Degree of precision, and reliability	low		high
Control over the response	low		high
Communication skill required	high		low
Opportunity to express feelings	high		low
Economical use of time	low		high

▬▬ = high   —— = medium   -- = low

Direct and Indirect Questions

The best way to get information may be to ask for it directly. There are some times, however, when a straightforward approach won't work, for example, when a supervisor's question, "Do you understand?" gets a "yes" from an employee who sincerely but incorrectly believes the "yes" answer. Even when able, a person may not be willing to give a direct answer if it is seen as risky or embarrassing. A boss who asks, "Are you satisfied with my leadership?" during an appraisal interview isn't likely to get a straight answer if the employee thinks the boss is unfair.

The following are some examples of direct questions:

Do you understand?

Are you satisfied with your new assignment?

Some examples of indirect questions are as follows:

Suppose you had to explain this safety policy to some other people in the department. What would you say?

Imagine that you were manager of this department. What kinds of changes would you make?

Hypothetical Questions

Hypothetical questions seek an answer to a "what if" situation. They can be useful for indirectly getting a person to describe beliefs or attitudes. For example, "If we were to take a poll about the morale level around here, what do you think the results would be?" Hypothetical questions are also a useful way of learning how another would respond in certain situations. "Suppose you became assistant safety manager and had to talk to one of your workers about needing to be more cautious on the job. What would you say and do if the workers accused you of acting bossy?"

Leading and Loaded Questions

A leading question either forces or tempts the other to answer in a specific way. Leading questions frequently include implicit or explicit references to the answer you expect. For example, "You don't mind working long hours, do you?" When a question virtually dictates only one acceptable answer, it stops being leading and becomes loaded. Some loaded questions use emotionally charged words and name calling to intimidate the other. "You haven't fallen for those worn-out arguments, have you?" Others rely on a bandwagon effect for pressure: "Do you agree with everyone else that it's best to put this incident behind us and forget the whole thing?"

Probe

A probe is usually used after an open question. A probe maybe a simple "Is that right?" "Really," "How so?" or "Tell me more." Using silence is an excellent technique for probing for more information.

Once you have determined the types of questions to use, you will need to organize them into a logical order so that the exchange flows smoothly and you get the information you need.

Arrange the Setting

Recall a time when you tried to persuade your boss to accept your new idea, but every time you began to explain yourself the telephone rang, interrupting the conversation. You can overcome such obstacles with advance planning.

Time

You can handicap yourself by choosing a time that is bad for you. We have all tried to cram a half-hour conversation into fifteen minutes before lunch, closing time, or an important meeting, or knowing we don't begin to think clearly until 9 A.M., we schedule an important breakfast meeting. Just as important as considering our timing is taking into account the needs of the other. One would be foolish to schedule an important exchange when your subject is rushed or preoccupied by some other important matter.

Location

The right place is just as important as the right time. Arrange a setting that is free from distractions. Holding calls is a good way to assure the attention of your partner. Sometimes it's best to choose a location away from the normal environment of either person. The chance of interruptions is lessened, and people may speak more freely and creatively when they are in a neutral space away from the familiar.

Pay attention to the way you seat yourself and the other person. The physical arrangement of the setting can also influence the exchange. Sitting behind a desk can emphasize unequal power and formality. On the other hand, a seating arrangement in which both face each other across a table or sit with no barrier between them encourages equality and informality, while increasing the amount of information exchanged. Distance, too, affects the information exchange. Sitting three feet apart will create more immediacy than sitting at a distance of six or seven feet. The choice of closeness or distance depends on your goal.

CONDUCTING THE EXCHANGE

Like most acts of communication, an exchange consists of three stages: an opening or introduction, a body, and a closing.

Opening

A good introduction can shape the entire exchange. People form lasting impressions of one another in the first few seconds of a conversation. These initial impressions influence how a listener responds to everything that follows. The opening is also a time to motivate the other to cooperate and give a sense of what will follow. An effective introduction includes greeting the other person, creating rapport, and giving an orientation about what will follow.

Greeting and Establishing Rapport

It is your responsibility to initiate the greeting. After the greeting, you need to establish rapport by initiating a light yet sincere conversation on a topic of interest to you both. The purpose is to help the other person relax. If you sense that the other person is nervous or anxious, take whatever time is required to help him or her feel comfortable.

It is during this time that the emotional tone of the exchange is set, whether it be formal or informal, nervous or relaxed, candid or guarded. Suitable topics for light conversation include a mutual friend or acquaintance, shared interests, job-related topics, or current events.

Orientation

Give a brief overview of what is to come. Resolving the unknown helps to put the other person at ease. At the same tme, it helps establish and strengthen your control. Begin by explaining the reason for the exchange, what information is needed, and how it will be used. Mention the approximate length of time required for the exchange. This will help the other person feel even more comfortable and will establish mutual expectations.

Consider ways to motivate the person you're speaking with. Persuade the other person to cooperate by promising recognition ("We're always open to better ways of running the department; we'd like to hear your ideas") or promoting the other person's concerns ("Choices you make about employee safety can involve hundreds, even thousands, of dollars over a single year").

Body

In the body, the questions and answers are exchanged. It is your responsibility to keep control of the conversation and the direction it takes. It is quite common to drift away from the agenda. Another loss of control occurs when too much time is spent in one area of discussion, thereby slighting another. Try to allot rough blocks of time to each agenda item and follow these guidelines during an exchange.

Some people get so wrapped up in the questions they are about to ask that they fail to fully listen to the answers. Note taking is helpful; however, excessive note taking may make the other person feel uneasy and prevent you from listening.

Be sure to correct any misunderstandings. Two strategies can boost the chance of getting your message across. The first involves restating. You restate both in the body and in the closing of the exchange. In addition, you can summarize important ideas in a memo before, during, or after the session.

Closing

An exchange shouldn't end with the last answer to the last question or "That's all I have." Several things must be addressed in the closing to bring the exchange to a satisfactory conclusion. Review and clarify the results. It is also important to clarify how the information received will be handled. You can establish an expectation as to future actions to be taken.

6
Employment and Appraisal Interviewing ▲

This chapter looks at two specific applications of the one-to-one communications skills covered earlier, the employment interview and the performance appraisal interview. Many managers are particularly uncomfortable in these settings, and usually, so is the other person.

THE EMPLOYMENT INTERVIEW

The short time spent in an employment interview can shape the lifetime of an applicant and the progress and financial status of the employer. More than ten million such interviews occur each year. In each one, the single most important factor in making employment decisions is the ability to communicate effectively. This ability has been found to be more important than work experience, personal appearance, grade point average, or extracurricular activities (Tschirgi, 1973).

The average manager spends roughly two thousand hours per year, or upwards of eighty thousand working hours, in his or her career. The emotional and financial results of poor employment decisions can be devastating. Popular opinion dictates that the employment interview is persuasive in nature, which is the reason why so many poor decisions are made. For this reason, the employment interview is best approached as an information-gathering and information-receiving interview.

When approaching the employment interview persuasively, the employer tries to convince the interviewee to take the job and join the company, and the interviewee tries to convince the employer to hire him or her. What typically occurs is that the employer glorifies the job and company and the applicant does the same with his or her background and experience. Because both employer and applicant have dressed up their positions so well, when they enter into an employment contract, both become disenchanted. The employer is disappointed because the new employee fails to live up to the employer's inflated expectations, and the applicant is disappointed because the company climate, morale, and the job itself reveal themselves to be less than glorious.

When approaching the employment interview as information giving and receiving, both employer and applicant can gain more realistic pictures of the job and the person and make better, well-informed decisions. Each has information to give and receive, as shown in Table 6.1.

**Table 6.1   The Employment Interview:
An Exchange of Information**

	Information to give	Information to receive
Employer	Overview of the company	Applicant qualifications
	Description of job	Applicant motivation
Applicant	Fitness for job	What the company is like
	Knowledge of company	Coworkers

The current statistics on employment interviews reveal that most interviewers are far too swayed by factors other than fitness for the job and are highly likely to make uninformed decisions. In one study, over 85 percent of the employment decisions were based on personal appearance and prior information about the applicant rather than results of the employment interview (Springbett, 1958). Without knowledge of the interviewing techniques presented in this chapter, employers may make decisions based on the impression the applicant gives rather than on the applicant's qualifications.

Research also shows that interviewers are more influenced by unfavorable information than by favorable. In other words, interviewers tend to look for reasons not to hire an applicant. The applicant who makes the fewest mistakes usually gets the job. Applicants go to great lengths to create a favorable first impression. Employers need to be aware of the "halo effect" and guard against such hasty decisions. One way to avoid this mistake is by using a structured interviewing approach. Decisions based on structured interviews are much more likely to be grounded on facts and qualifications rather than on first impressions.

In a survey of 153 companies conducted by Northwestern University, 79 percent of recruiters said their initial impressions influenced the rest of the interview and that clothing created the initial impression. The study also ranked the primary reasons that employers rejected applicants. Note that none of them pertain to qualifications for the job (Endicott, 1980). The reasons for the rejections are as follows:

1. Poor personal appearance

2. Conceit

3. Inability to express oneself clearly

4. Lack of goals

5. Indifference
6. Lack of confidence
7. Overinterest in money
8. Expectations that were too high
9. Excuse making
10. Lack of tact

These survey results reveal the importance of solid interviewing skills for the interviewer and the need to make sound decisions based on accurate information gathered in the interview.

Conducting the Employment Interview

If you are conducting an employment interview, approach the interview as suggested earlier in this chapter. Some particular steps apply to the employment interview.

Preparation

You will need to do some preliminary work to prepare for the interview. Determine your objective, which is usually to decide on the best applicant for the job. Review the job. Review the applicant's file. Note any particular questions you may want to ask based upon the information you have. Next, prepare the list of topics you plan to discuss. Standard topics for an employment interview include work experience, education, personality, and motivation.

Once you have determined the topics to discuss, determine how structured you want the interview to be. Do you have one hundred applicants and five interviewers to help you? If so, you will probably want to use a fairly structured interview so that all interviewers ask the same questions and receive accurate, dependable information. Once the screening interviews are completed, you can interview the final candidates yourself in a less structured interview. If you have a smaller number of applicants and the time to conduct the interviews yourself, you may want to use a less structured approach. This is to your advantage, because it will help the applicant to feel more relaxed and thereby give you more accurate information.

Developing Questions

Perhaps begin with an open question to encourage the applicant to talk. Follow the open question with a probe or perhaps a closed question. Or you may prefer the opposite approach—starting with a closed question to verify the applicant's length of work experience, for example, and then using an open question to encourage the applicant to elaborate. Avoid asking compound questions, such as, "Tell me about your education and work experience." Half of such a question will probably go unanswered. Now that you have the body of the interview planned, begin preparing the introduction and closing.

For the introduction, check the applicant's file for something you might be able to chat about to establish rapport. If you don't find anything, try a current event. Then decide what you will tell the applicant about what to expect in the interview. It is the interviewer's responsibility to help the applicant to feel comfortable. You might extend your hand for a handshake and offer something to drink.

For the conclusion, remind yourself to summarize the interview and to let the applicant know what steps will be taken next. Always allow the applicant an opportunity to ask questions and to add any information he or she wants. There may be something important that you have overlooked. By concluding in this way, you provide the opportunity for the applicant to show confidence and leadership ability, for the interviewee may then begin to close the interview.

The following table summarizes those questions that various laws, court rulings, and guidelines make illegal if asked prior to the employment of an applicant. In general, they include direct or indirect inquiries that would reveal sex, race, religion, age, or national origin, or those that concern matters having an unequal effect on various applicant groups. Table 6.2 gives examples of nonpermissible and permissible inquiries. It should be noted that these laws and rulings change often. Consult the proper authorities for an up-to-date listing.

Table 6.2   Permissible and Nonpermissible Employment Inquiries

INQUIRY AREA	NONPERMISSIBLE	PERMISSIBLE
Identifying Information		
Name	• Requiring prefix (Mrs., etc.) to applicant's name. • Inquiring into previous name of applicant whose name has been changed by court order or otherwise.	• First, middle and last name of applicant. • Other name(s) under which applicant may have worked or attended school, or may be known to reference.
Address	• Inquiring into foreign addresses which would indicate national origin.	• Applicant's address and telephone number, and alternative address and telephone number.

INQUIRY AREA	NONPERMISSIBLE	PERMISSIBLE
Identifying Information Address	• Inquiring into length of time at present address. • Inquiring as to whether applicant owns home, rents, rooms, or lives with relatives.	
Age	• Requesting date of birth or age prior to employment. • Requirement of birth certificate, baptismal record, etc., prior to employment.	• Inquiry of "are you under 18" may be used if desired. • Applicant may be requested to supply work permit from school authorities if question of underage exists. • Application may be requested to submit birth certificate or other proof of birth date *after* employment.
Sex	• Inquiry into sex of applicant.	
Marital Status	• Inquiry into marital status of applicant. • Inquiry into applicant's maiden name.	
Religion/Creed	• Inquiry into applicant's religious denomination or affiliation, church, parish, pastor, or religious holidays observed. • Applicant may not be told "This is a Protestant, Catholic, Jewish, etc., organization."	
Race/Color	• Any inquiry indicating race or color.	
Education	• Inquiry about the nationality, racial, or religious affiliation of schools attended by the applicant.	• Inquiries into academic, professional, vocational, etc., schools attended, courses studied, grades, etc.

(continued)

Table 6.2 cont.

INQUIRY AREA	NONPERMISSIBLE	PERMISSIBLE
Identifying Information		
Education	• Inquiry about applicant's date of high school graduation.	
Military Service	• Inquiry into applicant's general military experience or other than U.S. military service. • Asking location of local draft board. • Requiring applicant to produce copy of military discharge papers or discharge number. • Requiring applicant to indicate type of discharge.	• Inquiries may be made only for U.S. military service. • Were you dishonorably discharged? • Applicants will be required to submit U.S. military separation papers *after* employment.
Organizations	• General inquiry into organizations to which applicant belongs, or inquiry into organizations which may indicate applicant's race, religion, color, sex, national origin, or ancestry.	• Inquiries may be made about membership in those organizations which are not indicative of race, religion, color, sex, national origin, or ancestry.
Physical Characteristics		
Height/Weight	• Establishing minimum height or weight hiring requirements, and inquiries about height or weight.	• Inquiries into height and weight are permissible only if a legitimate job need for this information can be established.
Color	• Inquiries into color of hair, eyes, complexion, or color of skin.	
Photographs	• Any request for applicant's photograph prior to employment.	• Photographs may be requested after hiring if for a legitimate business purpose.

INQUIRY AREA	NONPERMISSIBLE	PERMISSIBLE
Physical Characteristics		
Physical Handicaps; Worker's Compensation	• Discrimination against the physically handicapped is unlawful if the applicant is able and competent to perform the duties of the job. Employing units should be aware that they are under an obligation to take affirmative action to employ and promote qualified handicapped and disabled veteran employees, including an obligation to make reasonable accommodations for such handicapped employees under Department of Labor Regulations issued pursuant to the Rehabilitation Act of 1973, and Vietnam Era Veteran Readjustment Assistance Act of 1974. • Have you ever received worker's compensation?	
Character		
Criminal Record	• Inquiries into arrests.	• Inquiries into convictions (except traffic violations).
Character Reference	• Asking from references, information about the applicant prohibited by any of the above nonpermissible inquiries.	• Applicant may be asked for references.
Relatives/Dependents		
Dependents	• Spouse's name inquiry. Inquiring about number or ages of applicant's children or other dependents.	• Relevant information about spouse, children and other dependents may be determined after employment.

(continued)

Table 6.2 cont.

INQUIRY AREA	NONPERMISSIBLE	PERMISSIBLE
Relatives/Dependents		
Relatives	• Inquiries about names, addresses, ages, etc., of any relative, spouse, or children. • Inquiry into location of relatives' places of business. • Inquiry into relatives currently or previously employed by the company.	
Emergency Notification	• Inquiry about name of relative, spouse, children, or other dependents to notify in case of emergency.	• Inquiring about name and location of *person* to notify.
Background Information		
Birthplace	• Inquiry Re: birthplace of applicant, applicant's spouse, parents, other relatives, children, or other dependents. • Requirement that applicant submit birth certificate, naturalization, or baptismal record prior to employment.	• Proof of birth or citizenship may be requested after employment.
National Origin	• Inquiring into applicant's lineage, ancestry, national origin, descent, parentage, or nationality. • Inquiry about nationality of applicant's spouse or parents. • Inquiry about applicant's "mother tongue" or how applicant acquired ability to read, write, or speak a foreign language.	• Inquiry as to languages which applicant can read, speak or write.

INQUIRY AREA *Background Information* Citizenship	NONPERMISSIBLE	PERMISSIBLE
	• Any inquiry into citizenship status which would reveal the applicant's lineage, ancestry, national origin, descent, parentage, or nationality. • Inquiry "Of what country are you a citizen?" • Asking whether applicant is a naturalized or native-born citizen, or the date when the applicant acquired citizenship. • Asking applicant's date of arrival in U.S. or port of entry. • Asking if applicant's spouse or parents are naturalized or native-born U.S. citizens, or asking the date when such persons acquired citizenship. • Requiring applicant to produce naturalization or first papers.	• Inquiries of "Are you a U.S. citizen?" and "If not a U.S. citizen, do you have the legal right to work/remain permanently in the U.S.?" • Proof of citizenship or birth or of legal right to work or remain in the U.S. may be requested after employment.

Source: Joseph Zima, *Interviewing: Key to Effective Management* (Chicago: Science Research Associates, 1983).

The list in Table 6.2 concerns *only* those inquiries that represent potential legal problems; it does not encompass many other possible employment inquiries. Thus, inquiries into type of position desired, work experience, employment record, job and career objectives, and numerous other frequently considered employment topics are assumed to be permissible if they do not appear on the list. However, care should be taken with these inquiries also, to assure that they are job relevant and do not concern potential race, sex, age, religion, or national origin issues.

The list in table 6.2 is designed to represent the most conservative approach to complying with all applicable rulings and regulations on employment inquiries, and variations are possible with respect to a few of these items. The corporate legal staff may be consulted to explore such variations if items on this list cause problems for an employing unit. Such contact, however, should be restricted to truly serious problems, for the range of permissible variations from this list is limited. Also, observance of these guidelines as they stand provides the best assurance of meeting legal requirements for employment inquiries and will contribute to improved consistency in employment practices across the corporation.

When you conduct the interview, you may want to take a few notes to help you later, but avoid writing too much, for it can make the applicant feel uncomfortable. Make sure your timing of the interview is good for you and the applicant. Avoid making the applicant wait for a long period of time, since waiting only serves to increase tension for the applicant. Set up the room in a manner consistent with your style and conducive to communication between the two of you.

Remember, as an interviewer you are not only trying to get accurate information, but you are also representing your company. The interview can be a source of public relations for the company. Each applicant will form an impression of your company and share that impression with others. Remember also that you are responsible for controlling the direction of the interview and that the interviewee should do most of the talking, or you won't get the information you need. Figure 6.1 summarizes the interviewing process in terms of "Dos" and "Don'ts." E in this figure represents the interviewee.

Figure 6.1   Some Employment Interview Dos and Don'ts

DO	DON'T
Prepare well.	Don't keep E waiting.
Plan length of time for interview.	
Hold all calls to avoid interruption.	
Dress well.	
Begin by introducing yourself.	
Smile.	Don't be too formal.
Make E feel comfortable in the room. Suggest a chair if more than one is available.	
Select a topic for discussion that establishes a common ground.	
Involve E in conversation as soon as possible.	
Create an informal homey atmosphere.	

DO	**DON'T**
Let *E* finish each answer before asking another question.	Don't rush the interview.
	Don't simply restate the application form.
Encourage *E* to do most of the talking.	Avoid asking too many questions.
Steer the interview to obtain *pertinent* information.	Don't let the interview get off the track.
Be prepared so you can give full attention to the applicant.	Avoid trick questions or discomforting ones.
Avoid unfavorable information.	Don't flatter *E* or offer false praise.
Acknowledge positive points *E* makes.	Don't steer the applicant toward answers.
Use language *E* will understand.	
Provide job requirements. If possible, show *E* what the job involves.	Don't exaggerate job opportunities.
Explain the company's operations; detail its products or services.	Don't promise things beyond your control to deliver.
Present the benefits your company offers.	Don't paint a false picture of the company.
Provide *E* with necesssary information to make an informed decision.	Don't pretend to know an answer that is out of your area of expertise.
Answer all questions fully.	
Keep notes.	Don't let notetaking appear too obvious.
Guard against the "halo effect."	Don't stereotype.
When the objectives are met, bring the interview to an end.	Don't drag out the interview.
Before closing be sure *E* has no further questions.	
Summarize the interview's major points.	
Let *E* know what happens next.	
If *E* is rejected, always explain why.	Don't mislead *E* with the promise of a job unless you are absolutely sure.
E should go away with a positive impression of you and the company.	
Immediately afterward, be sure to record all important information.	Don't trust that you will remember everything you discussed in the interview.
Be sure *E* receives any requested material.	

Source: Adapted from Joseph Zima, *Interviewing: Key to Effective Management* (Chicago: Science Research Associates, 1983), p. 182.

Being Interviewed for Employment

If you are interviewing for a position, there are some guidelines for you as well. Most important, remember that you are responsible for the success of the interview. You must show the employer that your background and experience fit the job for which you are applying. Two primary reasons that applicants are not hired are that (1) they can't show how their experience fits the job and (2) they think too highly of themselves (McBrearty, 1972).

Maintain the attitude that the employment interview is informative in nature. You are not just trying to persuade the interviewer to hire you. You are also there to see if the company and the job suit fit you. The first 30 seconds of the interview are the most crucial. This is when you create a first impression, so make sure that it is positive. Dress for the job or one step higher, as you can always remove a vest or loosen your tie if the company looks less formal.

Preparation

Research the company beforehand so that the employer knows you've done your homework. Develop three to five questions to ask the employer in the interview. These questions should imply motivation. Avoid asking questions about personal gain such as benefits, salary, vacation time, and the like.

Questions to ask include the following:

- What are the possibilities for advancement?
- Whom would I be working with?
- Do you anticipate expansion?

Other questions you might ask are listed in Figure 6.2, while Figure 6.3 indicates questions you may need to answer in an interview for a job.

Figure 6.2   Questions for *You* to Ask during Your Interview

Remember that the interview is a two-way street. While the employer will be attempting to ascertain your ability to do the job, you will also want to determine if the job is right for you. Consequently, you will want to have some questions, based upon your research of the employer, that you will want the interviewer to answer for you.

The questions you ask can also help to portray you in a favorable way to impress upon the interviewer your sincere interest and concern for doing a good job. To do this, the questions often need to be thought out in advance and be serious, probing queries that also indicate your knowledge of the employer and their interests and goals.

The following are a few basic questions which you may want to include with others that are tailored to the particular job:

1. Would you describe the duties of the job for me, please?

2. Could you show me where it fits in the organization?

3. What characteristics do you most like to find in people of this assignment?

4. Why is the position open?

5. What do you consider ideal experience for this job?

6. Who does my boss report to?

7. Was the precious incumbent promoted?

8. Could you tell me about the people who would be reporting to me? How does their pay compare with that in other sections/companies? Are you happy with their performances?

9. Is there anything unusually demanding about the job that I should know about?

10. What have been some of the best results produced by people in this job?

11. Could you tell me about the primary people I would be dealing with? What are their strengths and limitations as you see them?

12. What are the main results you would like to see me produce?

13. How much authority will I have over decisions?

14. Is there much turnover in this job area?

15. Why isn't this job being filled by someone within the company?

16. What are your biggest problems?

17. What do you like most about your company? Least?

Source: Frank Endicott and Peter R. Lindquist, *The Northwestern Endicott-Lindquist Report* (Evanston, IL: Placement Center, Northwestern University).

**Figure 6.3   Questions Frequently Asked during
Employment Interviews**

The purpose of an interview is for the interviewer to find out about you, the prospective employee. The employer wants to know about you in order to make a decision about hiring, and you want to present yourself in the most favorable light. Listed below are questions adapted from a survey conducted by Dr. Frank Endicott of Northwestern University and a few others. These are examples of questions asked by employers during interviews. Read the questions, role play the interview situation, and practice how you will answer them. A good interview often determines whether or not you get hired. Remember, nothing beats proper preparation.

1. In what type of position are you most interested?

2. What are your long-range and short-range goals and objectives, when and why did you establish these goals, and how are you preparing yourself to achieve them?

3. What specific goals, other than those related to your occupation, have you established for yourself for the next ten years?

4. What do you see yourself doing five years from now?

5. What do you *really* want to do in life?

6. Why did you choose your particular field of work?

7. How do you plan to achieve your career goals?

8. What are the most important rewards you expect in your career?

9. What do you expect to be earning in five years?

10. Which is more important to you: the money or the type of job?

11. Why do you think you would like this particular type of job?

12. What personal characteristics are necessary for success in your chosen field?

13. What do you consider to be your greatest strengths and weaknesses?

14. How would you describe yourself?

15. How do you think a friend or professor who knows you well would describe you?

16. What motivates you to put forth your greatest effort?

17. Why should I hire you?

18. What kind of experience do you have for this job?

19. What qualifications do you have that make you feel that you will be successful in your field?

20. How do you determine or evaluate success?

21. What do you think it takes to be successful in a company like ours?

Source: Frank Endicott and Peter R. Lindquist, *The Northwestern Endicott-Lindquist Report* (Evanston, IL: Placement Center, Northwestern University).

The Closing

As the interview comes to a close, after the interviewer has summarized and given you time to ask questions, take charge. Ask your questions, add any information that you need to, and request action. Ask for the job if you want it, ask when a decision will be made, and ask if you may contact the employer rather than wait for the phone to ring. Give the interviewer something to remember you by, such as another phone number, a business card, or work samples. Follow up on the results of the interview. A phone call or letter is most appropriate.

Eighty percent of the time, it is the closing of the interview that determines whether or not the applicant is hired. If an applicant is not hired, it is usually because he or she has not asked for the job. When you have found a position that you want, don't forget to ask for the job. One personnel director explained that an applicant may look and dress right, speak well, be qualified, and shine in the interview, yet not be hired. It is often a company's policy that no job offer be extended to an applicant who does not want the position badly enough to ask for it. Most companies want prospective employees to be enthusiastic about working for the company and about the responsibility that goes with the position. Most employers look for assertiveness and expect you to ask for the job under no uncertain terms (Thornton, 1989).

Difficult Questions

Oftentimes an interviewer will ask one of those "difficult questions." Let's consider a few of those hard-to-answer questions.

"Tell me about yourself."

If you are unsure what the employer is looking for here, simply ask for more specifics. If you start out with the day you were born, you may turn the interviewer off. By asking for specifics, you can find out if the employer wants to know about you as a person or about your experience.

"What is your major weakness?"

When answering this question, think about what the employer wants to hear. Then take one of your strengths and phrase it as though it were a weakness. For example, if you are a very detailed and organized person, try this: "I'm a stickler for details," or "I tend to get too involved in my work."

"What kind of salary are you looking for?"

It is a good rule of thumb to avoid discussion of salary in a first interview. There will be plenty of time for that once you get your foot in the door. For this question you might try asking the employer what the going rate is for such a position. This puts the burden back onto the employer and prevents you from responding with a figure that is too high or too low.

Your Impression

Employment interviews are critically important for even the most qualified applicant, for the person who receives a job offer is often the one who knows the most about how to get hired. Managing your impression is a critical factor in successful interviewing. Figure 6.4, a self-test, will help you assess your ability to manage your impression.

Figure 6.4   Self-Monitoring Test

The statements below relate to personal reactions to a variety of different situations. No two statements are exactly alike, so consider each carefully before answering. If a statement is true, or mostly true, as applied to you, circle the T. If a statement is false, or not usually true, as applied to you, circle the F.

1. I cannot easily imitate another person's behavior.	T	F
2. I like to impress or entertain people, so I put on a show.	T	F
3. I'd be a great actor.	T	F
4. People sometimes get the impression that I have strong emotional reactions when actually I do not.	T	F
5. I avoid being the center of attention in group situations.	T	F
6. I find that I adopt differing behaviors depending on the people or cirumstances I am in.	T	F
7. I must be sold on an issue or idea in order to argue for it.	T	F
8. I tend to react the way I think people expect me to so I will be liked and accepted.	T	F
9. Even if I dislike someone, I will pretend to be friendly.	T	F
10. I may behave at times quite unlike the person I really am.	T	F

Scoring: If you answered F to questions 1, 5, and 7, score one (1) point for each F. Score one (1) point for each of the remaining questions that you answered T. Add up your points. If you honestly scored 7 or above, you are probably a high self-monitoring individual; 3 or below, you are probably a low self-monitoring individual.

Psychologists refer to the strategies and techniques that people use to control the impressions they convey to others as *"impression management."* Some people are particularly sensitive to the ways they express and present themselves in social and professional situations.

Source: Adapted from Mark Snyder, "The Many Me's of the Self Monitor," *Psychology Today* 13 (March 1980): 34.

A study of 479 personnel directors found that the following four factors were most likely to lead to a candidate's rejection:

1. Lying, dishonesty
2. Alcohol on the breath
3. Rudeness or impolite attitude
4. Failure to demonstrate interest in the interview

     (Goetzinger, 1959)

Employment interviews are critically important for even the most qualified applicant, for the person who receives a job offer is often the one who knows the most about how to get hired.

PERFORMANCE APPRAISAL INTERVIEWS

The performance appraisal interview should accomplish several objectives. These include the following:

- Making sure the employee knows how he or she is viewed
    praise work well done
    point out areas that need improvement
    relay to the employee what future prospects are possible

- Communicating better and improving employee morale
    build good relationships between employee and direct superior
    enhance the feeling of employee participation in the job

- Seeing the employee's point of view
  encourage employees to express their opinions
  gain knowledge that will improve company operations
- Planning for the future
  define performance standards
  encourage employees to work toward those standards
  target employees for promotion

Both managers and their subordinates are frequently uncomfortable in the appraisal interview because most people find criticizing an unpleasant task, while being on the receiving end of the negative evaluation can be an ego-damaging experience. Therefore, appraisal interviews are often avoided or conducted poorly. Theoretically, appraisal interviews can be a valued management tool. Employees should know where they stand and how they can improve. One of the greatest needs employees have is to know where they stand with management. Receiving personal feedback correlates highly with job satisfaction (Downs, Berg and Linkugel, 1980, p. 106). In one study conducted by the Academy of Management, 90 percent of interviewees expressed satisfaction with their experience in the appraisal interview (Mayfield, 1980). In another survey, 87 percent of the interviewers and 71 percent of the interviewees regarded their appraisal interviews favorable (Downs, Berg and Linkugel, 1980, p. 106).

Criticism of Appraisal Interviews

Appraisal interviews can take many forms. As Zima (1983, p. 253) points out,

> Organizations vary widely on how they conduct their appraisal interviews. In some organizations there is no face-to-face meeting between boss and subordinate, while others have very elaborate peer-appraisal procedures. Some managers evaluate employees by marking a checklist on a rating form or writing a paragraph describing an subordinate's performance; supervisors may also consult with their bosses to assess a subordinate's performance. This is often done in the absence of the subordinate and without his or her input. These approaches are seriously deficient. Without employee input and a face-to-face discussion, the validity of the performance appraisal is seriously in question.

Effective appraisal interviews are vital to the smooth functioning of the entire management system. Poorly conducted appraisal interviews may produce a variety of negative results, including a demoralized work force, high turnover, apathy, complacency, misunderstandings, misdirected effort, hostility, and even sabotage (Meyer, 1974). Four major reasons can be cited for the failure of appraisal programs. First, managers resist appraisal programs because they find the role of judging others to be a difficult one. Second, the planning for the interview is often deficient and defective. Third, managers try to accomplish too many often contradictory objectives in one interview. Fourth, managers frequently lack the skills to conduct effective performance appraisal interviews (Zima, 1983).

General Electric conducted a study of appraisal programs focusing on the interview between employees and their managers, because this is the discussion that is supposed to motivate employees to improve their performance. The following interesting results emerged (Meyer, 1974, pp. 20–24).

1. Criticism has a negative effect on achievement of goals; defensiveness resulting from critical appraisal produces inferior performance.
2. Mutual goal setting, not criticism, improves performance.
3. Praise has little effect one way or the other.
4. Performance improves most when specific goals are established.
5. Coaching should be a day-to-day activity, not a once-a-year activity.
6. Participation by the employee in the goal-setting procedure helps produce favorable results.
7. Interviews designed primarily to improve an employee's performance should not at the same time influence a salary or promotion.

These results tend to indicate that day-to-day managing skills are more important in improving performance than the annual appraisal interview. Coaching needs to be an informal, frequent occurrence, not a formal annual ritual. Praise or criticism of performance in the course of daily on-the-job contacts is expected by the employee and does not take on exaggerated importance.

Studies and experiments demonstrate the need for an appraisal system with the following characteristics (Burke and Wilcox, 1969, p. 293):

1. Periodic and frequent meetings between manager and subordinate during which progress is reviewed, problem solution is sought, and new goals are established
2. A high level of subordinate participation in the appraisal and development process

3. The mutual setting of specific goals to be achieved in the future
4. A helpful and constructive attitude, rather than a negative one, on the part of the manager
5. The solution of job problems that may be hampering the subordinate's job performance.

Format and Procedure

Concentrate on job-related standards. Disagreeing over traits such as character, attitude, and personality is very easy, whereas arguing with job-oriented standards is difficult. The following are some examples of job-oriented employee performance standards:

Percent increase in profit	Number of customer complaints
Amount of sales	Number of parts produced
Number of new accounts generated	Attendance record
Work projects completed on schedule	Safety record
Percent reduction in accidents or absenteeism	Maintenance of equipment
	Amount of line downtimes
Quality index	Keeping accurate inventories
Amount of scrap material produced	

Concentrating on job-related standards is results-oriented and considerably more supportable than evaluating someone's personality.

Advance planning is necessary. Before the interview make sure that you do the following:

Notify the employee ahead of time, allowing him or her adequate time to prepare for the appraisal.

Keep ongoing records of the employee's performance in specific, measurable terms.

Examine the employee's written job description if one exists.

Familiarize yourself with the employee's previously established job objectives.

Make certain that the employee has been thoroughly familiar with the evaluation criteria.

Allow employees sufficient notice and time to evaluate their own performance and prepare any feedback they will need.

After the interview, review the evaluation and make your assessments of the employee's performance (Zima, 1983, pp. 253–255).

Phases of the Performance Appraisal

Once again, the appraisal interview has an opening. After an initial exchange of pleasantries, the supervisor provides a rationale for the interview, an outline of what information is needed and how it will be used, and a preview of the interview's probable length. The body of the interview ought to include the following three steps:

1. Define criteria. Identify the criteria by which the employee is being evaluated. Ideally these criteria will already be clear to both management and the employee, since they were established at the previous appraisal session. In any case, it is wise to restate them.

2. Evaluate performance This is easiest when the goals are measurable: Are accidents down 10 percent? Have jobs been completed on time? Of course, the employee might have explanations for why targets were not reached, and it is the supervisor's job to consider these fairly.

   When goals are subjective, the evaluation of performance will be more a matter of judgment. Try to turn vague goals like "being more patient" into simple behavioral descriptions such as "letting others talk without interrupting them."

   Without meaning to let it happen, a manager and employee can become involved in discussing a relatively unimportant point at length. It's better to attend only to key areas. A skillful interviewer will focus on the most important criteria, usually no more than three topic areas.

   The evaluative nature of the appraisal interview can provoke defensiveness in some employees. Previous chapters have described behaviors that are likely to increase defensiveness and contrasting behaviors that can help reduce feelings of threat. A supervisor who uses supportive styles of communication keeps the odds of defensiveness as low as possible.

3. Set goals. The next phase is to define goals for the future. The goals need to meet five criteria:

   - Goals should cover whatever areas of the employee's performance are important: both relations with others and job-related behavior.
   - Goals should focus on a few important aspects of the job. The tried and true 80/20 rule applies: changing 20 percent of a worker's behavior usually solves 80 percent of the problems.
   - Goals should be described as specifically as possible so that both manager and employee will know what actions constitute successful performance.

- A time period needs to be established for each target. People often work best when faced with a deadline, and set dates let both parties know when the results are due.
- The targets ought to provide some challenge to the worker, requiring effort yet being attainable. A manageable challenge will produce the greatest growth and leave workers and managers feeling pleased with the changes that occur.

(Downs, Berg, and Linkugel, 1980)

After the interview, the manager might complete a final report that summarizes the results of the interview. The employee can have the option of adding his or her own response to the manager's report. This document then can become part of the employee's records, to be used as a basis for future evaluations and promotion decisions.

Appraisal Don'ts

The following list describes what *not* to do during appraisals:

- Don't discuss personalities. Concentrate on job-specific behavior.
- Don't soft-pedal valid criticism. It isn't fair either to the employee or to the organization to leave the impression that criticisms are not important.
- Don't compare the employee to others. Holding someone else up as a model will probably not have a positive impact on the employee's ability and willingness to improve.
- Don't use the sandwich technique of alternating praise and criticism. The result is that the praise seems insincere and the criticism is emphasized.
- Don't criticize employees for things beyond their control. The injustice of this will cause them to ignore valid criticism you may have.
- Don't argue about an evaluation. Express your opinion with an explanation of the reasons behind it. Redirect the conversation toward what can be done to improve performance.

(Zima, 1983, p. 266)

Problem Solving in the Performance Appraisal

When approaching the appraisal as a problem-solving interview, the manager and employee work together to define areas of concern and develop appropriate solutions. Thus the manager becomes less a judge and more a coach.

Problem-solving interviews are built on the idea of mutual interest and a win/win orientation. Both parties realize that their best interests are served by cooperation and that alternative solutions are available that will satisfy them both. While the appraiser retains the power that comes with a managerial position, boss and employee work together in a cooperative manner so that neither orders nor threats are necessary. Adler (1983, p. 167) describes some keys to success in problem-solving interviews. "Several elements are essential if a problem-solving approach is to succeed. First, there must be mutual respect and a genuine desire to come to a common solution. The employee's attitude is equally important: a defensive worker could interpret even the most sincere desire for cooperation as a kind of manipulation and threat. Besides having the right attitude, both need to listen well in order to understand the other person's position."

The performance appraisal gives superiors and subordinates a structured way to look at the quality of the subordinate's performance. When conducted skillfully, they are welcomed by most employees as a chance to learn how they are viewed by management.

7
Conflict ▲

List the words that come to your mind when you hear the word "conflict." Chances are, you list some of the responses we often hear:

fights	win or lose	anger
disagreement	hostility	violence
war	competition	

Most of us view conflict as negative. This response is natural. We wouldn't think of listing words such as exciting, strengthening, creative, stimulating, helpful, or innovative. While conflict should be associated with these words, society has reinforced a view of conflict that is primarily negative.

Most of our assumptions about conflict come from our childhood. Several cliches present a fairly clear picture of how we were raised to view conflict. "If you can't say anything nice, don't say anything at all," "Pick on someone your own size," and "Children should be seen and not heard" reflect socially approved views of conflict. Rarely do we learn how to handle conflict productively (Wilmot and Wilmot, 1978). In work and social settings we learn to conform to the expectations of our peers. "Try to get along," "Don't rock the boat," and "Don't make waves" are very familiar messages which imply that conflict is to be avoided.

ORGANIZATIONAL REWARDS

When we begin our careers in organizations, we quickly learn that we will be rewarded for compliance and conformity to organizational values. We are not rewarded for effectively dealing with conflict. As a result, employees assume that they have limited choices in dealing with conflict. Seldom are we encouraged to generate conflict or use it to gain information and respond to change. Fear or anxiety about conflict can lead to conservatism and conformity. This phenomenon is based on the fear that conflict will result in severe negative consequences for participants and therefore one should go along with others for fear of ridicule or dissent. The result is a decrease in the effectiveness of decisions and lack of creativity. Yes-men do not challenge, and well-informed, rather conflict-shy subordinates seldom make the valuable contributions they are capable of.

CONFLICT IN CHANGE: A NECESSARY CONDITION

Conflict is inevitable, often predictable, and an integral part of change. Change is not only healthy, it is necessary. One cannot avoid conflict, because it is a natural byproduct of human communication. Conflict promotes growth, the new development of new information, and increased understanding. Conflict can increase energy and motivation. When we compete, we tap and mobilize energy that otherwise would not have been available to us. We spend a tremendous amount of effort in order to win, to get that promotion, or to be on the winning team, which ultimately benefits the organization. In the absence of conflict there is potential for stagnation, since employees take fewer risks and squelch their creativity.

One of the reasons for our negative view of conflict stems from the way we often deal with conflict. When conflict consumes so much of one's energy or resources that little is left for task accomplishment, it is destructive. Unmanaged conflicts can interfere with work and interpersonal relations, creating hostility and antagonism. Another reason for our negative view of conflict results from the belief that one person must win and the other lose. This happens when two people compete for the same job, the same resources, or the same title. In such an atmosphere we become very cautious. Others are perceived as "enemies" and those involved may attempt to keep others from gaining an advantage or information. Information becomes a source of power over others rather than a shared resource.

ELEMENTS OF CONFLICT

There are three elements that create conflict. They include expectations, roles, and power.

Expectations

Expectations are seeds for conflict and govern how we view a conflict. In short, we see what we expect to see. For instance, you and a coworker learn about a job opening that would provide a pay increase and more challenge. You think your coworker is going to compete against you for the position. You act on that expectation and compete against your coworker. Later your coworker asks you why your relationship has changed, and you learn that he or she had no intention of applying for the position. A good rule of thumb to follow is to check out your perceptions when you are in doubt.

Hidden agendas and unstated expectations naturally set you up for conflict. Let's say you want to be considered for a promotion. You expect that the boss will naturally think of you first, but you never make that expectation known to your boss. When the position is given to another, you become upset and disappointed, and you may even blame or ridicule your boss or the company. Unless you make your expectations known, there is no sure way to get them met. It is much more effective to take personal responsibility for meeting your expectations by telling your boss that you would like to be considered for the promotion. Taking personal responsibility for your expectations can help you attain your goals and prevent unnecessary conflict.

Roles

Roles are created because of the demands and expectations placed on us by other people. A role not only affects our behavior but it affects the way we perceive other people's behavior. Roles also affect the way we perceive ourselves. Roles influence and direct our communication behavior. The nature of communication in organizations is that it involves a number of people simultaneously negotiating roles and meanings with others. Therefore, numerous potential problems can seriously influence the effectiveness of communication and the development of productive relationships with others.

One of the difficulties with roles is that you may fill many of them, and often several at a time. The person who gets promoted to a supervisory position and now must be boss to those who were formerly his or her peers may be confused about which role to play when dealing with employees. Role conflict exists when one set of expectations about how you should play a role conflicts with another set of expectations. Such conflicts may have several sources.

Conflict arises when you receive inconsistent directives from the same person or several people on how to do something. For example, a huge amount of work is expected, and you must do it quickly. Conflict occurs when different people send expectations that conflict with one another. For example, a worker knows it is crucial to get the work out to satisfy the customer. The boss has given an almost impossible deadline. He has also said that he will accept no accidents and that no shortcuts are allowed.

Role overload is present when the expectations others have of you outweigh the amount of energy, time, and skill you have to fill them (Myers and Myers, 1985). Your boss may expect you to work overtime on a special project to meet a crucial deadline, your spouse may expect you home early to attend an important engagement, your child may insist that you keep a promise to attend the last game of the season, and your instructor may have assigned several articles to be read and reported on at the next meeting of your night course. The conflict here is in terms of the sheer quantity of what is expected of you in the various roles you perform.

Conflict also occurs when somebody expects you to do things that are quite out of character for you (Myers and Myers, 1985). There are times when you may be expected to do certain things that do not fit your self-concept. If you see yourself as a compassionate person, it will be difficult for you to fire someone, particularly when the person to be fired may have great difficulty in finding another job, has five children to feed, is a single parent, and so forth. Yet your supervisory position may require that you let that person go.

Still another form of conflict occurs when nobody tells you clearly how you are expected to act. The blue collar worker is told the company values quality work, yet he or she is paid by quantity. Managers are told to use new and creative ideas yet are also told they must fit in. Students are told they are in class to learn, yet their work is graded.

If not managed well, interdepartmental relations have the potential for generating conflict. As competition increases, the potential for conflict increases. Within each department, task accomplishment takes precedence over organizational goals. Quality control tries to keep rejects to a minimum, industrial engineers try to expedite work flow standards, research and development aims for sophistication and elegance, while the line manager tries to simplify tasks. These tasks conflict, yet all are considered in resource allocation. As a result, each department advances its own cause and competes for management favor.

Due to roles in the organizational hierarchy, compliance is expected. Any potential conflict naturally goes underground and could blow up at any time. Those in top management control the behavior of others and allocate resources according to goals as they see fit. As managers focus on predictability and control for planning and allocation of resources, they expect employees to accept certain orders and rules. As a result, employees counter management by trying to increase their own autonomy. Most organizations have finite resources, and allocation of those resources has a direct bearing on each employee's life. When more resources are allocated to an employee, the employee's sense of power increases. When allocated resources are reduced, the allocation is never seen as fair from the employee's standpoint. Perceptions of injustice are seeds for conflict.

Power

Power is usually unequally distributed in organizations. The more resources you have, the more power you have. As your accumulation of resources increases, so does your power to interfere with another's goal attainment. As a result, persons in less powerful positions often experience frustration and seek to form coalitions to combine strength to meet with a more powerful party. This results in conflict. Successful managers anticipate this and seek remedies to prevent such conflict.

Persons with high authority tend to use coercion. Their ways are forced upon those lower in authority, which limits freedom of action. Lower-level employees try to gain retribution wherever possible. Each member attempts to exercise influence and control, making it impossible to communicate without exerting influence.

CONFLICT STRUCTURE

You can understand how conflict works by looking at games. In most games, the results of your moves depend upon the other player's moves. A game is structured by the choices you make and the payoffs you receive for your choices, which are made according to agreed-upon rules (Wilmot and Wilmot, 1978). If you can change this structure, you can alter the conflict that you are in and the power you have. Making choices involves obtaining information about the situation so that you can select alternatives. In making choices there is always a degree of uncertainty regarding the following variables:

1. The other's perception of your moves
2. Your perception of the other's moves
3. What payoffs you will receive from your moves
4. What payoffs the other will get from his or her moves

Without the rules as laid out in a game, how do you determine what alternatives the other will have to choose from in a real-life conflict situation?

- You can ask the other party.
- Observe the other's behavior in similar situations.
- Assume that you are in the other's place and predict what your choice would be.
- Guess about uncertain rules of behavior in such circumstances (not knowing whether the other party will follow the rules).

(Wilmot and Wilmot, 1978)

The workplace contains many opportunities for game playing.

> For instance, take the case of two business colleagues who both have a chance for a prestigious promotion. Their friendship is important to them. They make a pact saying it's alright to compete for the job, and no matter who wins, they will still be friends and support each other. Party A thinks he will win anyway, and does not think through how he will feel if party B wins. Party B gets the promotion after some competitive tactics. Party A switches by saying, "A true friend wouldn't have treated me that way. Our friendship will never be the same." Because the relationship is important, the guilt motive becomes important, the winning party is had, and party A can say, in essence, "I've Got You, Now." The hidden payoff was punishment for the loser to exercise over the winner. (Wilmot and Wilmot, 1978, p. 79)

Still another example of a game, or attempt at controlling the structure of a transaction, is "Damned If I Do, Damned If I Don't," in which the structure is set such that your options are limited, you will be punished for any choice you make, and it is impossible for you to leave the situation. The result: you cannot not choose. For instance, after an employee makes an error and is injured, if he doesn't report it, his manager says, "Next time tell me about it, so we can remove the hazard, and it won't hurt you or how I view your performance." When the employee makes the next error and reports it to his manager, the manager responds, "Now you really blew it. I knew you'd screw up again. Now you've ruined our record—we were less than 30 days from a new record." By telling his boss about his mistake, the employee loses his job. By not telling his boss about his mistake, he will tarnish his boss's perception of his performance. The worker needs his job and does not have the immediate option of joining another firm. Also known as the double bind, this is a common game.

CHARACTERISTICS OF CONFLICT

While conflict is an ongoing sequence of events involving expectations, roles, and goals, the only way of identifying conflict is by behavior. To determine whether a conflict actually exists, look for the following characteristics:

- Observable behavior
- Dependence on others
- Expressed difference of opinion
- Frustration
- Signs of stress

Observable Behavior

You can detect conflict by looking for some type of observable behavior. It is usually some sort of expression of struggle. Whether it be slamming a door, a sarcastic comment, or an argument between two people, the struggle must be expressed in such behavior for conflict to exist.

Dependence on Others

Conflict requires that the persons involved are interdependent. You may be independent in some ways, yet dependent on each other to achieve your goals or accomplish a task. When you choose a particular goal or task, due to the nature of the interdependent relationship, you affect the other's ability to choose.

Expressed Difference of Opinion

When conflict exists, you and another person perceive that your goals are incompatible and the rewards are scarce. The key word here is *perceive*. Some goals are compatible, and some rewards are bountiful. Each person's perception contributes to the conflict situation. If we know that rewards are scarce, we will attempt to frustrate the other in pursuing the reward.

Frustration

When someone intrudes into your territory, you feel threatened. An interdependent relationship can place the other in a position to interfere with your goals. We tend to react to such frustration by choosing destructive action against the other. We often choose destructive goals (setting out to block or hurt the other) when our own goal does not appear possible. Some people become so accustomed to not achieving their goals that they adopt a repetitive destructive stance toward others. The frustration over not accomplishing goals becomes internalized and frozen into a concept that the goal of relationships is to "get the other." In destructive conflict, your attitude changes from concern over the initial issues to concern over not yielding.

Signs of Stress

The list of stress signals shown here, although not complete, provides some clues about behaviors displayed by a person experiencing high levels of stress. These behaviors are the ones most frequently identified as being signals of stress by participants in several stress management workshops. When any of the following signals appear as new behaviors, they are probably signs of high levels of stress:

1. Disregarding low- or high-priority tasks.
2. Spending a reduced amount of time on each task.
3. Adjusting boundaries to shift or avoid responsibilities.
4. Blocking out new information.
5. Being superficially involved; appearing to give up.
6. Expressing negative or cynical attitudes about customers or clients.
7. Appearing depersonalized, detached.
8. Going "by the book."
9. Being overly precise; intellectualizing.
10. Displaying inappropriate humor.
11. Stealing or using other means of "ripping off" the organization.
12. Obviously wasting time; being unavailable much of the time.
13. Being late or frequently absent.

(Adams, 1980, p. 174)

In conflict situations, we are torn between the desire to compete for what we want and the desire to cooperate (Wilmot and Wilmot, 1978). This situation almost always causes attendant stress. In the next section we will explore how we balance the need to compete and the need to cooperate when dealing with conflict.

COOPERATION VERSUS COMPETITION

In each conflict we face, we must decide whether to cooperate or compete, or how to balance each need. Our choice will most definitely affect the outcome, as can be seen in the following example.

Figure 7.1   Game Board

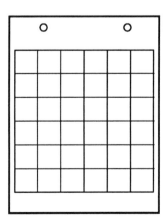

Pretend you and a partner have been told you are going to play a game similar to tic-tac-toe, using a grid like the one in figure 7.1. You are told that your goal is to win the game. Each party will have ten seconds to place his or her mark in the chosen square. The game is over when all the squares have a mark in them. To win you need to have three rows (horizontal, vertical, or diagonal) of five squares marked with your symbol.

You flip a coin to see who marks first; let's say you win. Consider your first move. Where will you place your X? Let's say that you put your X in the upper left-hand square. Now consider your opponent's move. He or she places an O directly next to your X in an attempt to block you. You proceed to make your next mark, and the process continues until all the squares are filled, with you marking and your opponent blocking. At the end of the game, you both discover that neither party has three rows of five marks. Our research with this simple game has shown that at least nine out of ten times, neither party is likely to win this game until after it has been played several times and carefully thought through.

With regard to cooperation and competition, this exercise is very revealing. Your partner's choice to immediately block your progress sends you a message that competition is the name of the game. You respond in turn, and so on and so on. In reality, there are a total of 36 squares, and only 30 squares are needed for both sides to be able to win (3 rows × 5 squares × 2 players = 30). How, then, might both go about winning? The answer lies in cooperation. If each party keeps to his or her own side of the game board and trusts that the other will cooperate, both parties can and will win.

8
Managing Conflict ▲

CONFLICT MANAGEMENT STYLES

We develop a variety of styles for managing conflicts, styles we prefer to use because they seem to work or because they fit our personality. We also develop relational styles for managing conflicts for the same reasons. We develop styles for reasons that make sense to us. No one style is automatically better than another, and each style is appropriate for certain situations. Our styles undergo change as we adapt to the demands of new situations.

When we can change and adapt our styles, we are more likely to be effective in managing conflict and achieving our goals than when we avoid change. Effective communicators expect change and adapt to change in their communication with others (Hart and Burks, 1972). By practicing a variety of styles, you will view others' behavior more rationally and be less likely to judge it.

In order to make effective choices about how to manage conflict, the first step is to understand your present conflict style. In every conflict situation, you struggle with two competing forces: concern for self and concern for others—in other words, cooperation and competition. There are five conflict management styles: avoiding, competing, accommodating, compromising, and integrating (Kilmann and Thomas, 1975). These styles are best understood by examining the diagram presented in Figure 8.1.

As illustrated, when avoiding conflict, you are not concerned about your own goals nor those of the other. The avoider refuses to engage openly in conflict. You may sidestep the issue by changing the subject or simply withdraw. Avoiding can serve its purpose in some situations; however, it does not prevent the conflict from happening. This is usually the least effective style of conflict management. It results in "I lose, you lose."

Figure 8.1   Conflict Management Styles

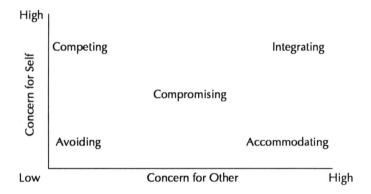

Source: Ralph H. Kilmann and Kenneth W. Thomas, "Interpersonal Conflict-Handling Behavior as Reflections of Jungian Personality Dimensions," *Psychological Reports 37* (1975), 971–980.

If your style is competing, you are concerned about your own goals and have very little concern for the other. The competitor pursues self-concerns at the expense of the other. By competing you attempt to gain power, using direct confrontation or trying to win the argument without adjusting to the other's goals and desires. The competitive style can be used appropriately when you openly compete to accomplish your goals without having a negative effect on the other. This style results in "I win, you lose."

When accommodating, the opposite of competing, you are not concerned about your own goals, and you cooperate with the other. The accommodator neglects self-concerns in order to satisfy the concerns of the other. You might obey the other's directives when preferring not to do so, or you might yield to the other's point of view. Accommodating is appropriate when you realize that the other's goals are more important, or your relationship is more important than what you are pursuing. This style results in "You win, I lose."

Compromising is midway between concern for self and concern for the other. The compromiser holds beliefs such as "You have to give and take," "You win some, you lose some," and "Not everyone can get their own way." While compromising addresses issues in conflict, sometimes compromisers give in too easily and fail to find a solution that satisfies both parties. Compromise results in "We both win and lose."

When your high concern for reaching your own goals is moderated by a high concern for the other, you are using an integrating style. You work creatively to find new solutions that will achieve both parties' goals. Integrating results in "I win, you win."

RELATIONAL STYLES

Your predominant conflict style usually changes with different conflict situations. You may compete on the job, avoid with your parents, and compromise with your spouse. It is hard to be consistent among relational styles because we learn patterns that allow us to adjust to the other persons involved. Our relationships also influence our conflict management styles.

There are three basic types of relationships: complementary, symmetrical, and parallel (Lederer and Jackson, 1968). In a complementary relationship, you choose styles that complement each other. For instance, if you are competing, the other accommodates. In a complementary relationship you adopt a style that works with the other's style.

On the other hand, as the Wilmots (1978, p. 40) explain, "In a symmetrical relationship you both strive for control in the relationship. If two co-workers both use an integrating style, then the similarity of their styles builds up a symmetrical system. In a symmetrical relationship you can walk away feeling a great deal of understanding for each other. Sometimes, however, striving for the same type of control can lead to unhealthy competition or one-upmanship."

Finally, the parallel relationship offers the most options, because "in a parallel relationship you develop flexibility depending on what the situation calls for. In a parallel relationship, your styles do not become rigid; they change to meet the demands of each conflict situation. Parallel relationships often offer the best chance for growth and change" (Wilmot and Wilmot, 1978, p. 40).

INCREASING YOUR POWER

The following are guidelines for increasing your power in a conflict situation:

1. Listen carefully to what the other person says. Take notes, clarify, answer questions, and maintain eye contact.
2. Give the best explanation possible. The best explanation considers both parties' points.
3. Be prepared to prove what you say. Have your facts ready.
4. Be prepared to talk in detail, even if it means repeating the same information.
5. Stay calm. Even if you feel angry, try to present yourself in a rational and positive attitude.

6. Assure the person that your goal is to solve the problem and not to hurt him or her. You do this by offering alternatives.

7. Show that other competent and respected persons have made choices similar to the ones you propose.

8. Make promises about future dealings to let the other know that you propose to operate in good faith.

9. Let the other person know you are aware of the advantages and disadvantages of a variety of outcomes.

(Wilmot and Wilmot, 1978, pp. 61–62)

MANAGING CONFLICT FOR PRODUCTIVITY

You have a choice in how you manage conflict. As one author team relates, "Just as in games of strategy, in each conflict you choose how you want to handle the conflict. You have four strategic choices. You may decide you want to avoid the conflict, maintain it as it is, reduce it or even escalate it. Strategies direct conflict and are the overall game plans in conflicts. Tactics are the moves we make to push the conflict in the direction that we want" (Wilmot and Wilmot, 1978, p. 104).

Avoiding the Conflict

Do you tend to avoid conflict? If so, you're not alone. "Avoidance is a common strategy for coping with conflict. We often use it in the first stages of a new relationship. Avoidance can lead to productive or destructive conflict. When it is overused and there is never any escalation, relationships become static and growth is not likely. Avoiding is appropriate when you can gain nothing by confronting, when power is drastically unequal or when you want to distance yourself from the other" (Wilmot and Wilmot, 1978, p. 114). There are many ways to avoid conflict, as shown in Figure 8.2.

Figure 8.2   Conflict Tactics: How to Avoid Conflict

- Refuse to recognize it
- Put it off
- Make rules
- Play with space
- Label the event
- Force agreement
- Use fogging

Source: Joyce Wilmot and William Wilmot, *Interpersonal Conflict* (Dubuque, IA: William C. Brown, 1978).

Refusing to Recognize the Conflict

You can refuse to recognize the conflict. This is sometimes a productive technique if you are in a high power position. It can, however, be a painful, disconfirming experience for the other. Often in the desire to avoid a conflict through refusing to recognize it, you create larger ones.

Putting It Off

You can avoid the conflict by setting a later time for it. The following dialogue is an example of destructive postponing:

Jim: I'm so upset. Why did you do that?
John: Can't we talk about this tomorrow?
Jim: It's fine for you to say that. You don't have to deal with it.
John: Look, I'm running late and I don't want to talk about it.

By this time Jim is probably angry not only about John's behavior but his refusal to talk about it. An example of putting off conflict productively follows:

John: I know you're upset, Jim. I also feel bad. I'm very late and
        don't have time to deal with all the issues now. When I return
        to work tomorrow we'll discuss the whole thing.
Jim: You always say that, and nothing ever happens.
John: This time it will. We'll sit down over coffee and the two of us
        can talk. I know you're upset.
Jim: Well, OK. I know you have a lot to do before that.

Putting it off works best when emotions are acknowledged while referring to discussing the issues at a later time. It is important that you agree on a time that is soon and realistic. The other must believe that you really mean to bring up the issue later. It's not appropriate to put it off when you have energy and a desire to work out the conflict right away.

Making Rules

You can structure the process by which important decisions will be made. By setting up the rules you gain power in a conflict. While deciding what to discuss, you can assess power, form coalitions if necessary, and determine what the level of involvement is. For example, you might say, "What shall we discuss tomorrow at the staff meeting?" or "Before we leave I want to settle upon the topics to be covered by this committee."

Playing with Space

Sometimes you can move closer to the other to intrude on his or her personal space so that conflict might be less likely. You can also avoid the person by leaving the scene. When you are outnumbered, physically threatened, tricked into being present for a conflict in which you do not wish to participate, or unwilling even to maintain physical presence for some reason, walking out can be effective, as long as you are willing to take the consequences for the action.

Labeling

You can label or redefine the conflict. Label yourself, the other person, or the conflict itself to avoid the conflict. For example, you could say, "I'm really not up on all of the issues here; give me some time to look into this," "Look, you're in charge of marketing; let me get marketing's view," or "This is not an issue we can solve today."

Forcing Agreement

You can use force to escalate a conflict and also to avoid conflict temporarily. Forced agreement only deals with half of the issues. Instead of gaining willing acceptance, agreement is forced. Bribes and emotional blackmail fall into this category.

Fogging

Fogging is a useful tactic when you are in a low power position or do not want to engage in conflict. Instead of replying to criticism or demands for change, fog by agreeing with part of the criticism but choosing to ignore the rest of it. If overused this can become dangerous. An example follows:

Bob: Your department is slipping up on the schedule.
Jane: They sure are busy, I'll look into it.

Maintaining Conflict

There are times when it makes sense to maintain conflict. "Maintenance tactics neither reduce nor escalate conflict, but keep it at a level of tension that motivates change. Maintenance tactics allow both parties to gain something by keeping the conflict going. They can promote fair dealings between parties for the issues at hand and when appropriate, promote effective conflict management" (Wilmot and Wilmot, 1978, p. 133). Figure 8.3 shows how to sustain conflict.

Figure 8.3   Conflict Tactics: How to Maintain Conflict

- Trade
- Issue a thromise
- Establish ground rules

Source: Joyce Wilmot and William Wilmot, *Interpersonal Conflict* (Dubuque, IA: William C. Brown, 1978).

Trading

Trading consists of getting something for something. It is basically compromise. The key to a successful trade is that you treat the other as equal in order to make the trade.

Issuing a Thromise

You can also maintain a conflict by issuing a thromise, a combination of a threat and a promise. The thromise is a message that combines escalation with reduction.

Example: "I can only stay with a company that allows me equal participation in decisions."

Establishing Ground Rules

Establishing ground rules helps maintain the intensity of the conflict so that you are motivated to manage it.

Example: "OK. It's difficult for me but I'm going to stay here and talk with you until we find out what the problems between us are."

Escalating Conflict

Intensifying conflict also has its benefits. "When you escalate a conflict involvement increases, issues are sharply defined, the number of issues increases and parties polarize. Escalating involves an attempt to place more pressure on the other to change, instead of changing the nature of the relationship. Escalating involves asserting force on the other by threatening to act or acting independently of the other's wishes, while relying on your interdependence as a condition to help bring the other into line. Escalation is appropriate when the stakes are high and quick resolution is critical" (Wilmot and Wilmot, 1978, p. 123). Ways to escalate conflict are listed in Figure 8.4.

Figure 8.4   Conflict Tactics: How to Escalate Conflict

- Make a mountain out of a molehill
- Form a coalition
- Use threats
- Limit access

Source: Joyce Wilmot and William Wilmot, *Interpersonal Conflict* (Dubuque, IA: William C. Brown, 1978).

Making a Mountain out of a Molehill

Making a "mountain out of a molehill" by expanding issues and bringing up related topics makes it clear to the other party that more is at stake than just the expressed issues. The following dialogue is an example.

Supervisor:	Did you clock in?
Employee:	Of course I did.
Supervisor:	Did you turn in your report yet? My secretary says she never received it.
Employee:	Don't you think I can do anything right? First it's arriving to work, then it's my report. You don't trust me to do a good job, do you?

Forming a Coalition

You can form a coalition by appealing to others to join your cause and assist you in attaining your goal. This tactic increases your power. Coalition formation is an attempt to shift the power balance between parties. As a manager you can make sure meetings include everyone involved in decision making so that the need for coalitions will decrease.

Using Threats

You can use threats when you are willing to inflict punishment or harm on the other in order to achieve your goal. Threats focus attention on what each of you has to lose rather than on cooperative elements and thus escalate the conflict (Swingle, 1970). A threat can only be issued by a source who can control the outcome, for instance, an employer who says, "Get with the program and work harder or you will be laid off."

Threats can be effective in generating change in the other party. The silent treatment is a nonverbal threat. The negative reactions that threats bring can be used to help create a sense of relief when they are discontinued. You cannot use threats productively unless the person being threatened believes that your threat is credible. A threat is credible only if you are in a position to administer the punishment and appear willing to invoke it and the punishment is something to be avoided. Threats escalate conflict and build power, but they cannot by themselves resolve conflicts.

Limiting Access

You can constrict the amount of time you will give to the other to be heard. This can be frustrating and cause the person to fight harder for a hearing. Limiting access of the other person to you reduces the person's power and frequently produces hostility and escalation.

Reducing Conflict

For any number of reasons, you may want to scale down conflict. "Reducing conflict . . . shows others that conflict does not have to be destructive and that you can express differences without hurting the relationship. In a healthy relationship a variety of reduction patterns are used" (Wilmot and Wilmot, 1978, p. 136). See Figure 8.5 for a list of these techniques.

Figure 8.5   Conflict Tactics: How to Reduce Conflict

- Break down the issues
- Use negative inquiry
- Talk about communication
- Address the issue
- Compromise
- Establish criteria

Source: Joyce Wilmot and William Wilmot, *Interpersonal Conflict* (Dubuque, IA: William C. Brown, 1978).

Breaking Down the Issues

You can reduce conflict by breaking down issues. Break conflicts down into several smaller, more manageable conflicts.

Negative Inquiry

You can use negative inquiry. When you are criticized, respond by asking for information about what it is that the other person finds objectionable. Then try to solve that part of the problem that is solvable. An example is as follows:

Boss:	I want to meet with everyone here for a private conference. People are spending too much time on coffee breaks and not getting their work done.
Worker:	Have you been unhappy with some part of my work?
Boss:	I can't think of anything right now.
Worker:	How do you think I might improve my work?
Boss:	Perhaps by doing a bit more research on problems.
Worker:	I understand.

By asking for more information, you reduce the conflict. Be sure you really want the negative information; you could get more than you bargained for.

Talking about Communication

Talking about your communication can reduce conflicts. Your credibility is enhanced by showing that you are a person of goodwill who can see all sides of a problem. This safe period of talking gives the other enough information about your reaction to the conflict so that he or she will be more aware of additional alternatives.

Addressing Issues and Emotions

You can reduce conflict by asking the other to present facts as well as feelings to give you information about the conflict in terms of both the issues involved and the relationship itself. If you consider only the facts, you might never reach resolution of an issue loaded with emotional content.

Compromising

Compromise reduces more conflict than any other tactic, especially when parties view compromise as a situation where everyone can win and lose something.

Establishing Criteria

Agree ahead of time on the decision-making process (e.g. voting) that is going to be used or on the criteria for making choices. If disagreements arise, the manager can point to the outside criteria. If you can agree on criteria, you usually can agree on the final choice.

EFFECTIVE CONFLICT SKILLS

Effective conflict management depends on your interpersonal communication skills. In addition to the skills discussed elsewhere in this book, use the following guidelines to improve your conflict management ability (Filey, 1975):

- Describe rather than evaluate. Describe behavior and your reaction to it rather than labeling the other person. For example, "This is the third time this week you've punched in after eight" instead of "You are always late."
- Be specific. Feedback is more effective when it describes specific instances instead of general feelings. Try to avoid using such phrases as "most people," "they say," "it seems we," or "one might think." If a statement is worth making, it is worth making specifically so the impact can be felt and the specific information needed is obtained.
- Focus on what can be changed instead of givens. Saying "There's nothing I can do to change that" is not very helpful. Concentrating on things that cannot be changed is a waste of time and emotional energy.
- Give feedback as soon as possible. Feedback loses its effectiveness if you say, "I was angry at your suggestion at our last staff meeting. I thought about it all week." Feedback has more impact if given closer to the actual event.
- Speak for yourself. Use "I think" or "I feel," indicating ownership of your thoughts and feelings.
- Summarize and get commitment. It is crucial to gain commitment at the end of the discussion. An effective conclusion involves (1) summarizing where you have been and what has been decided, (2) asking and probing to see if there are any unresolved issues or concerns, and (3) asking for clear commitment to the resulting action items. Without commitment your effort could be wasted.
- Establish superordinate goals (goals that are more significant than the conflict issue). Superordinate goals are usually based on some need to cooperate. Meeting a profit target, reducing costs, and winning a contract are examples of superordinate goals.
- Equalize power. When the balance of power is grossly unequal, you can equalize the power so that both parties are better able to manage the conflict. One of the ways to bring about a power shift is to help the other to understand the costs incurred by his or her behavior. A shift in the balance of power allows both to more effectively deal with one another. Being somewhat equalized, both will feel that

what they say and do will make a difference and will work harder toward a solution.

- Create an outside adversary. Membership in an organization provides acceptance and belonging to employees and enables the organization to get commitment to organizational goals and motivation to work through the pressure to conform to organizational values. Likewise, establishing an outside adversary can strengthen loyalty and commitment, leading employees to value their goals over the adversary. Using an outside adversary can provide excitement and motivate employees to adhere to organizational goals.
- Provide rewards for effective conflict management. In organizations, winners of conflicts have a tendency to become "fat and happy"; tension is released and the desire to work decreases. There is little desire to explore earlier conflicts and learn from them. Winning groups become even more cohesive. Losers of conflicts deal with losing in one of two ways: (1) they deny reality, saying they didn't really lose and claiming a moral victory or (2) they seek a scapegoat and blame rules or others for the defeat.

In order to prevent a win-lose conflict situation, you can do the following:

- Emphasize total organizational effectiveness and each employee's contribution to it.
- Reward and measure contributions as a total effort, not individually.
- Use a superordinate goal that all can support.
- Use frequent communication and issue rewards on the basis of the help one group gives to another group.
- Share rewards equally.

Balance cooperation and competition between employees and departments to achieve organizational goals and increase productivity and quality. Through creative staffing, you can provide for more productive conflict management. You can rotate employees. This helps employees to have empathy for other employees. You can also emphasize pooling resources to maximize organizational effectiveness.

YOUR OWN CONFLICTS

In your own conflicts you may wish to have a third party intervene; however, this may be impractical or unpopular with the other party. To manage the conflict, you have three possibilities:

1. Try to change the behavior of the other party or parties. When you try to change the behavior of others you persuade and motivate the other to change.
2. Try to change the structure of the conflict. All conflicts are structured around choices and potential payoffs for parties. Changing the game can give you more options than you thought you had.
3. Change your own behavior. Perhaps you will need to change your own behavior. You might change your behavior or your perceptions. Changing your own behavior requires insight. The following questions may be helpful in analyzing your role before deciding to change: What role do you play in the conflict? Try to identify patterns of interaction that recur. Are there any themes that tend to emerge time and time again? How satisfied are you with your role?

(Wilmot and Wilmot, 1978)

A CHECKLIST FOR MANAGERS

Do you tend toward productive or destructive conflict? The following questions will help you decide:

1. Do you respect the other's point of view?
2. Are you open to new ideas?
3. Do you approach conflict situations attempting to solve a problem?
4. Do you express your feelings and thoughts assertively?
5. Do you take time to respond to the statements made by the other?
6. Do you try to find a creative way to meet the other's needs rather than winning at the other's expense?
7. Do you treat the other with the same respect and accord you expect for yourself?
8. Do you strive to reach agreement *and* enhance the relationship for future communication?

If you answered yes to the above questions, you probably find productive outcomes from the conflicts you face.

9. Do you go to great lengths to win the conflict, including manipulating, using hostile language, and game playing?
10. Are you defensive and judgmental toward the feelings and thoughts of the other?

11. Are you so anxious to respond with your own point of view that you do not fully listen or respond to the other?

If you answered yes to questions nine through eleven, you may want to review your intentions and determine whether you're getting what you want.

9
Conducting Effective Meetings   ▲

In a study of fifteen corporations, researchers gave pocket recorders to a variety of key employees—from sales representatives to vice presidents—and asked them to list what they did every twenty minutes on the job. An analysis of almost 90,000 working days showed that an impressive 46 percent of the time was spent in meetings. Typical executives spend an average of ten hours per week in formal committee meetings and an additional seven hundred hours per year in other types of meetings (Coleman, 1983, pp. 35–43).

PROBLEMS WITH MEETINGS

Meetings can be a superior vehicle for communication; however, in other cases they can be quite counterproductive. Surely at one time or another you have been frustrated by a poorly run meeting. Some problems with meetings include wasted time, domination over the meeting by a few, and poorly formed decisions. Safety meetings, for instance, have been an integral part of almost every safety program. In most cases, they are considered by employees to be either worthless, boring, or counterproductive.

Meetings can also take up a considerable amount of time. In addition to the socializing that accompanies the meeting, time is spent waiting for everyone to arrive and in discussions that have little to do with the purpose of the meeting. By the time those present debate the pros and cons of an idea, considering every aspect, their decision may be too late or ill formed.

In most meetings, there is one individual who comments on every detail. This can be disruptive. Excessive talkers can get the meeting off track, resulting in poorly made decisions. Getting off track often results in arguments about trivial issues. While groups have potential for making superior decisions, they also have the capacity to make serious mistakes. Committees often adopt the decisions supported by their most talkative members, even though there's no guarantee that the biggest talkers have the best ideas. Group members may be unable to reach consensus on an issue and wind up settling for hasty compromises that satisfy nobody and accomplish nothing.

Another cause of poor group decisions comes from too much agreement rather than too little. In very close-knit groups, members tend to submit to pressure. Statements such as "Let's not rock the boat" and "I think we're all in agreement on that" indicate that the group members are on their way to making a poor decision. This tendency can be prevented by bringing in outside members for advice and opinions as a check on the quality of the decision being made (Janis, 1972).

While poorly run meetings produce poor results, well-managed meetings are well worth their effort. They produce more solutions than individuals, and the solutions are likely to be better than those made by individuals alone. Meetings also generate commitment—when members identify with the group, when they are involved in making decisions, and when their input is used. If you are leading a meeting, allow members to work out a solution together; they will feel it was their plan, not yours, and will work harder to implement it. Group members are more likely to support decisions they have helped to develop than decisions handed down from the boss. When employees take an active role in making important decisions that they are responsible for carrying out, their morale increases, there's a decrease in internal conflict, employee turnover, accidents, and absenteeism, and productivity rises.

A group may meet to solve a problem or make a decision. In such meetings the group decides to take some action or make changes in existing policies or procedures. Problem-solving and decision-making meetings are the most challenging type of meeting. In some meetings the social function is far more important than any specific task. These meetings serve several important purposes. They reaffirm the members' commitment to one another and to the company, and the sessions provide a chance to swap useful ideas and stories that might not be appropriate during work. This social communication can be invaluable, and the informal meeting provides a good setting for it.

IS A MEETING NECESSARY?

Successful meetings need to be planned in advance. The most important question is whether or not even to hold a meeting. Some issues are better handled one-to-one and over the phone or face-to-face. In fact, meeting at the wrong time can lead to serious problems. To determine whether a meeting is necessary, ask yourself the questions in Figure 9.1.

Figure 9.1   Is a Meeting Really Necessary?

1. Does the task or decision to be made require more than one person?
2. Are individuals or tasks interdependent?
3. Is there more than one alternative to choose from?
4. Are misperceptions or hesitations likely?
5. Do several people need to accept the solution before it is implemented?

Does the task require more than one person?

It might call for more information than one person has or it might take more time than one person has.

Are individuals or tasks interdependent?

Each member in the meeting should have a different role. Some can serve as information givers and some as listeners, reality checkers, or diagnosticians.

Is there more than one alternative to choose from?

Questions that have only one right answer aren't appropriate for discussion in meetings. Tasks that don't have fixed outcomes are appropriate for discussion.

Are misperceptions or hesitations likely?

Only by talking them out can members accept a solution. Often a meeting is the best way to gain a greater degree of understanding or cooperation.

Do several people need to accept to the solution before it is implemented?

One of the most important functions of meetings is to acquire support for a solution.

THE NEED FOR AN AGENDA

In a meeting without an agenda, those attending don't know why it's been called, why they're there, or where they're headed. A good written agenda contains the time, length, and location. Agendas also need other items.

The size of the group is important. Optimum size is five to seven. An odd number of members makes tie breaking easier if needed. In larger groups, the likelihood of some members becoming silent increases. It's best to keep the size small so that everyone can participate in discussions. Be sure to identify the people who will be attending on the agenda. By listing who will attend, you inform all members about whom to expect in the meeting.

Sometimes participants need background information to give them details or provide a description of the meeting's significance. A clear list of topics and goals helps members prepare. The best goals are results-oriented, specific, and realistic. Notice the difference between the following two examples: "To improve order processing efficiency" and "To develop a list of ways to shorten order processing cycle time." Specific goals also help to keep the discussion on track.

CONDUCTING THE MEETING

The best meetings occur when people are prepared. While it may look as though meetings require little effort, quite the opposite is true. Effective meetings require advance preparation in addition to important communication skills.

Beginning the Meeting

Effective openings get the meeting off to a good start, give everyone a clear picture of what's to be accomplished, and define what the group will do to reach its goal. Start the meeting on time. It does a manager no good to make employees wait until he or she arrives, since waiting for the manager only frustrates employees. It is better to be there early to welcome participants. The first five agenda items should be as follows:

1. Identify meeting goals.
2. Provide background information.
3. Tell the members how to participate.
4. Indicate the meeting format.
5. Identify time constraints.

Encouraging Participation

If the group leader does most of the talking, the meeting becomes a lecture rather than a group discussion. To encourage participation, you can ask questions of members. Your questions need to be open-ended, brief, simply worded and focused on only a single point. There are several ways to encourage participation.

1. Direct a question toward the group as a whole, with anyone free to answer. For example, "Accidents have increased in the past six months. Does anyone have an explanation?" If a few people start to dominate, then switch to another type of question.
2. Aim a direct question at a particular individual. For instance, "How would you solve that problem, Bill?" Use direct questions skillfully. Never start a discussion with a direct question, since it creates a classroom atmosphere and suggests that members shouldn't speak unless called upon.
3. Refer a question back to the person who originally phrased it. For example, "Suppose the decision were up to you, Greg. What would you do?"
4. Refer a question asked by one member to the entire group. For example, "John has just raised a good question. Would anyone care to respond to it?"

Keeping on Track

You may need to steer the direction of the meeting, particularly because when time is limited members often waste time in random discussions or bring up topics that are unrelated to the immediate issue. You can get the meeting back on track by using one of the following techniques.

Remind the group of time constraints.

Remind everyone about the importance of moving quickly. When doing so, it's important to acknowledge the value of comments being made by saying, for example, "Using posters sounds good, but for now we'd better stick to the newsletter program. Tom needs to meet with us at three, so we'd better finish this meeting within the next few minutes."

Summarize, and then redirect the discussion.

You can get the discussion on track again by tactfully summarizing what's been accomplished and mentioning the next task, as follows: "We've come up with a good list of the factors that might be contributing to accidents. Can anyone think of additional causes? If not, let's move on and try to think of as many solutions as we can."

Challenge the relevancy of ideas.

Unrelated ideas may be good ones that just don't apply to the group's immediate task. In other cases, they're not only irrelevant but useless. In either situation, you can get the group back on track by questioning the idea's relevancy. Ask a member to explain how an apparently off-the-track idea relates to the group's task, as in this example: "I'm confused, Tom. How will renting new equipment help us to reduce accidents?" At this point the member who made the original remark can either explain its relevance or acknowledge that it wasn't germane. The advantage is that it isn't taken personally because the question focuses on the idea and not the person. This should prevent the person from becoming defensive. Your question about the relevancy of a remark has to be sincere. If your tone of voice, facial expression, and other nonverbal cues suggest that the question is sincere, you can expect a calm reaction.

Promise to deal with good ideas later. Another way to keep the goodwill of a member who has brought up an irrelevant idea is to suggest a way of dealing with it at the appropriate time, for example, "That rental idea sounds promising. Let's bring it up to Jeff after the meeting and see what he thinks of it." One way to show your sincerity is to specify exactly when you'd like to discuss the matter, which might be a specific time or whenever certain conditions are met. Another way to show your sincerity is to inquire about the idea after the meeting.

CREATING A POSITIVE CLIMATE

In meetings, getting along can be especially tough when others don't cooperate with your efforts to keep the meeting on track or, even worse, attack your ideas. The following suggestions can help get the job done and keep a work group motivated.

Paraphrase and ask questions.

Criticizing can produce defensive reactions that could generate ill will. It's also important to remember that even a seemingly simple remark can have some merit. Handle such comments by asking for clarification, for example, "Why do you think we ought to sell the equipment?" You can also paraphrase to get more information: "It sounds as if you're saying we need more money." By paraphrasing, you can check your understanding and invite the other person to explain the idea in more detail.

Enhance the value of comments made.

Acknowledge ideas by praising or thanking the people who contribute them. You can also use praise for poorly presented ideas. Even comments that seem worthless at first often have some merit. Take advantage of these merits by following these three steps:

1. Acknowledge the idea.
2. Add your own comments.
3. Build on the idea by asking others for suggestions.

PRODUCTIVE PROBLEM SOLVING

A positive climate, balanced participation, and on-track discussions may keep your meetings pleasant, but by themselves they don't guarantee productive solutions to a problem. Meetings have the best chance of producing quality solutions when you use the problem-solving steps shown in Figure 9-2.

Figure 9.2   Productive Problem Solving

1. Define the problem.
2. Analyze the problem.
3. Establish criteria for a solution.
4. List possible alternative solutions to the problem.
5. Identify the best alternative.
6. Develop an implementation plan.

1. Define the problem.

Sometimes the problem facing a group is clear. It doesn't take much deliberation to understand what's necessary when the boss tells you to work out a vacation schedule for the next six months. On the other hand, some problems need redefinition because they are too narrow or too broad to be addressed, as in the following examples:

Too Narrow
Should we replace the punch press with the new model?

Better
How can we get our large-volume jobs done most quickly? (Sending them out to a job shop may be a better alternative.)

Too Broad
What can be done to reduce employee accidents?

Better
What new orientation programs would reduce accidents among new employees? (This approach suggests where to look for the nature of the problem and solutions.)

2. Analyze the problem.

List the causes, specify the effects, and describe the extent of the problem. If there is time, make sure to be comprehensive in your analysis.

3. Establish criteria for a solution.

Determine what conditions need to be met in order to solve the problem. Consider the criteria of all parties who will have to accept or evaluate the solution.

4. List possible alternative solutions to the problem.

Create a wide number of ideas from which members will eventually choose the best one. A widely used method for boosting creativity is brainstorming. This approach has four critical rules:

- Do not evaluate or criticize ideas.
- Encourage wild and crazy ideas.
- State the goal: quantity, not quality.
- Seek modifications or additions to previous ideas.

5. Identify the best alternative.

Review the list of solutions and evaluate each one based upon how well each fits the criteria.

6. Develop an implementation plan.

Work out an action plan or, at minimum, the next steps necessary to get the ball rolling.

ENDING THE MEETING

The way a meeting ends can have a strong influence on how members feel about your meeting and how well they follow up on any decisions made or instructions given.

When to End a Meeting

There are three times to end a meeting, as follows:

1. At closing time. When meetings run over, the cause is usually failure to follow the guidelines already mentioned in this chapter, resulting in off-the-track comments, digressions into personal attack and defense, and poor decision making. Even if the dis-

cussion has been a good one, close on time to prevent members from drifting off to other commitments, losing attention, or becoming resentful. Press on only if the subject is important and the members seem willing to keep working.

2. When you need more resources to continue. If the group lacks the necessary person or facts to continue, adjourn until the resources are available. Be sure to identify who is responsible for getting the needed information, and set a new meeting date.

3. When you finish the agenda. It seems obvious that a meeting should adjourn when its business is finished. However, some discussions drag on because no one is willing to end the meeting.

How to End a Meeting

When it's time to end a meeting, follow these three steps. In leaderless groups or in groups with a weak leader one or more members can take the initiative.

1. Indicate to the group that time is about up. This procedure allows the group to wrap up business and gives everyone a chance to have a final say. For example, the leader might say, "We have about fifteen minutes before we need to adjourn. We still need to hear Bob's report on the safety conference, so let's devote the rest of our time to that."

2. Summarize the meeting's results and future actions to be taken. Review the information gathered and the decisions that have been made. Remind members of their responsibilities and action items. A leader could wrap up the meeting as follows: "This has been a productive meeting for us. We will meet again at the staff meeting next month. Before then Jane will contact the customer and Bob will follow up with Barbara."

3. Thank the group. Acknowledge the group's efforts and individual contributions. For instance, a manager could conclude, "We accomplished a lot today. Thank you for attending. Brian, I appreciate the work you did for us. You certainly helped us out today."

FOLLOW-UP MEASURES

Don't assume that a meeting is a success until you follow up to make sure that you achieve the desired results. Follow-up involves the following four steps:

1. Document the meeting: items of agreement and action items.
2. After the meeting create an agenda for the next meeting. When meetings are held on a regular basis rarely are all items discussed in one sitting. Note which items need to be carried over from the last meeting.
3. Follow up. You can be sure that the promised outcomes of a meeting actually occur if you follow up with other members. If tasks were assigned, check on whether they're being performed. A friendly phone call or personal remark can do the trick: "Is the new phone system working for you?"
4. Follow up on your own assignments. If you wait until the last minute before tackling them, the results are likely to be inaccurate and possibly embarrassing."

GETTING MORE OUT OF MEETINGS YOU ATTEND

The following list suggests eleven ways to make sure you get the most out of meetings that you attend.

1. Carefully study the agenda in advance to determine which issues are a must and which speakers are those you would like to hear. Develop a well-organized schedule.
2. Sit with people you don't know, if possible. Friends and colleagues tend to distract each other with conversations not always relevant to the reason they are there.
3. Keep your mind open to new suggestions.
4. Remove all prejudices toward the speaker. Don't let them detract from the new ideas you might gain.
5. Take notes to provide a permanent record for future reference.
6. Ask questions if they are called for in the meeting. It is estimated that more than 50 percent of a typical group wants to ask a question but is too timid to do so.
7. Contribute to the proceedings. In an open discussion, many in the group fail to speak up because they don't want to give away their ideas. Invariably, this is a mistake, because ideas generate ideas.
8. Summarize your notes and be sure to get the names, phone numbers, and addresses of speakers whom you may need to contact later for more information.
9. Report what you have gained to others in your organization so that all may profit from your observations.

10. Apply what you have gained.

11. Follow up with minutes or documentation of agreements.

Figure 9.3 contains an inventory designed to pinpoint the roles you play in small-group meetings. It includes a score sheet and a discussion of each role.

Figure 9.3   Group Leadership Behavior

Instructions: Each of the items below describes aspects of group leadership behavior. Respond to each one according to the way in which you would be most likely to act if you were a part of a problem-solving group. Circle the letter to the left of the statement that best describes your likely behavior, noting that the letters signify: (A)lways, (F)requently, (O)ccasionally, (S)eldom, and (N)ever.

When I am a member of a problem-solving group . . .

(A) (F) (O) (S) (N) 1. I offer facts, give my opinions and ideas, and provide suggestions and relevant information to help the group discussion.

(A) (F) (O) (S) (N) 2. I warmly encourage all members of the group to participate, giving them recognition for their contributions, demonstrating receptivity and openness to their ideas, and generally being friendly and responsive to them.

(A) (F) (O) (S) (N) 3. I ask for facts, information, ideas, and feelings from other group members to facilitate any discussion.

(A) (F) (O) (S) (N) 4. I try to persuade members to analyze constructively their differences in opinions and ideas, search for common elements in conflicting or opposing ideas or proposals, and try to reconcile disagreements.

(A) (F) (O) (S) (N) 5. I propose goals and tasks in order to start action within the group.

(A) (F) (O) (S) (N) 6. I try to relieve group tension and increase the enjoyment or group members by joking, suggesting breaks, and proposing fun approaches to group work.

(A) (F) (O) (S) (N) 7. I give direction to the group by developing plans on how to proceed with group work and by focusing members' attention on the tasks to be done.

(A) (F) (O) (S) (N) 8. I facilitate communication among group members by showing good communication skills and by making sure that what each member says is understood by all.

(A) (F) (O) (S) (N) 9. I pull together related ideas or suggestions made by group members and restate and summarize the major points discussed by the group.

(A) (F) (O) (S) (N) 10. I ask members how they are feeling about the way in which the group is working and about each other as well as share my own feelings about group work and the way the members interact.

(A) (F) (O) (S) (N) 11. I coordinate group work by showing relationships among various ideas or suggestions, pulling ideas and suggestions together, and incorporating activities of other individuals.

(A) (F) (O) (S) (N) 12. I observe the process by which the group is working and use my observations to help examine the effectiveness of the group.

(A) (F) (O) (S) (N) 13. I determine why the group has difficulty in working effectively and what blocks progress in accomplishing the group's goals.

(A) (F) (O) (S) (N) 14. I express group standards and norms and the group goal in order to make members constantly aware of the direction in which the work is going—the progress being made toward the group goal—and in order to get continued open acceptance of group norms and procedures.

(A) (F) (O) (S) (N) 15. I energize the group by stimulating group members to produce a higher quality of work.

(A) (F) (O) (S) (N) 16. I listen to and serve as an interested audience for other group members, weighing the ideas of others and going along with the movement of the group when I do not disagree with its actions.

(A) (F) (O) (S) (N) 17. I examine how practical and workable the ideas are, evaluate the quality of alternative solutions to group problems, and apply decisions and suggestions to real situations in order to see how they will work.

(A) (F) (O) (S) (N) 18. I accept and support the openness of other group members, reinforcing them for taking risks and encouraging individuality.

(A) (F) (O) (S) (N) 19. I compare group decisions and accomplishments with group standards, measuring accomplishments against goals.

(A) (F) (O) (S) (N) 20. I promote the open discussion of conflicts between group members in order to resolve disagreements and increase group togetherness.

Score Sheet

Instructions: 1. If you circled (A) give yourself 5 points; (F) is worth 4, (O) is worth 3, (S) is worth 2, and (N) is worth 1 point.
2. Add your scores in each column to obtain totals in task and maintenance leadership functions.

Task Functions	Maintenance Functions
_____ 1. Information and opinion giver	_____ 2. Encourager of participation
_____ 3. Information and opinion seeker	_____ 4. Harmonizer and compromiser
_____ 5. Starter	_____ 6. Tension reliever
_____ 7. Direction giver	_____ 8. Communication helper
_____ 9. Summarizer	_____ 10. Evaluator of emotional climate
_____ 11. Coordinator	_____ 12. Process observer
_____ 13. Diagnoser	_____ 14. Standard setter
_____ 15. Energizer	_____ 16. Active listener
_____ 17. Reality tester	_____ 18. Trust builder
_____ 19. Evaluator	_____ 20. Interpersonal problem solver
_____ Total for task functions	_____ Total for maintenance functions

Task Maintenance Grid

Instructions:
1. Locate your task score on the horizontal axis of the grid and extend a vertical line to the top of the grid.
2. Locate your maintenance score on the vertical axis of the grid and extend a horizontal line to the point of intersection with your task line.
3. Place an "X" at the point of intersection to represent your two scores.
4. Determine which number combination best represents your style.

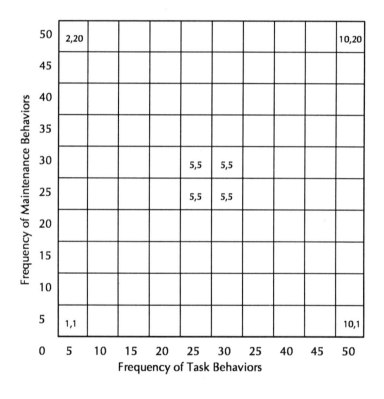

Key to Group Leadership Styles

(1,1)   Default
        You exert minimum effort to get the required work done and involve yourself little with other group members. You may rely on others in a passive way and choose not to feed into any conflict that exists. You might think to yourself, "To heck with it all!"

(1,10)   Good Neighbor
        You place high value on keeping good relationships within the group. You give much attention to others' needs in order to create a comfortable atmosphere and work tempo. You may have trouble getting work accomplished.

(10,1)   Self-Sufficient
        Getting the job done is important to you over and above good relationships. You may even overlook some group members. Group productivity could suffer due to low morale.

(5,5)   Traditional
        You balance the need to get the job done and have satisfying relationships. You continually make sacrifices to meet both needs and may neglect to seek or find creative ways to meet all needs for optimal productivity.

(10,10)   Eye-to-Eye
        All group members plan and make decisions together, and all are committed to getting the job done as they build relationships of trust and respect. You value sound, creative decisions that promote understanding and agreement. Ideas are sought out and listened to even when they differ from others. The group cooperatively defines the task and works for its completion. You encourage the creative integration of task and relationship needs and are a good leader for a group.

10
Management Presentations
that Make a Difference ▲

Almost every job requires well-organized professional management presentations. As the level of management rises, more formal and informal presentations are required. Often your company's image is affected by your ability to present yourself in front of others. Successful managers require good presentation skills, whether for conducting a safety meeting, disciplining an employee, or selling a proposal. Motivating employees requires mastering presentation skills needed to sell the program, explain the policy, or rally others behind a concept. If your presentations are disorganized and unprepared, you cannot be effective.

YOUR STAKE IN PRESENTATIONS

Every time you communicate, you influence others, whether intentionally or unintentionally. You communicate many things you may not intend to communicate. You are not always aware of what you communicate, and you may not always be understood.

When presenting yourself you need to be intentional and make use of all the tools available to influence others and create the response you desire. Such tools include your choice of words, the organization of your ideas, supporting materials, voice, gestures, audiovisual aids, the room layout, and dress. By using these to best advantage, you can increase the chances that you will get the response you desire from your audience.

A survey of 2,800 executives conducted by the American Management Association revealed that the ability to sell one's ideas was the number one requirement for success. The following are some important reasons for presenting yourself well.

- When you present yourself in public, your reputation is at stake.

  When you write you have the opportunity to edit and revise. When you speak, you must do it right the first time. Any error is stored in your listeners' memories and could be used against you. This means that you must learn to control what you say and how you say it.

- Each presentation gives you an opportunity to gain support or cooperation.

  Presentations not only help you sell an idea, they also help you control your message for the greatest impact. By doing this you will appear to be credible and reliable.

- In many organizations, the ability to present yourself well is a determinant of advancement.

  Executives observe their employees to discover those with a command of both oral and written communication. Those who appear responsible, accurate, and considerate are the ones selected for advancement. If you can win genuine approval, you can achieve relatively permanent success.

THE COMPETENT SPEAKER

The competent speaker wields influence in an organization, so presentation skills are well worth learning. "In order to get people around you to regard you as competent and worth listening to, you must motivate them by skillfully addressing their interests. If you appear well organized, present useful information and address your listeners' concerns, they will very likely accept what you have to say." (Phillips, 1982, pp. 50–52). To become a competent presenter, use the following guidelines:

- Make sure the idea is worth talking about.

  The idea should address the needs or interests of your audience. It can result in new information, a fresh interpretation of old information, an evaluation of important issues, a unique way of doing things, a question that will prompt people to make an intelligent decision, or a statement that will make people feel good about themselves or motivate them to do something well.

- Make sure the idea is supported with relevant information.

  The best way to support a good idea is to back it up with evidence and intelligent reasoning. Be prepared to justify your opinion and present examples to illustrate your points.

- Organize your thoughts clearly.

  In presenting your idea be clear, concise, and unambiguous, so that your listeners can understand and remember what you say.

- Emphasize important points.

  You are responsible for getting your listeners to listen. Listeners should respond by being polite. You need to control the volume of your voice so you are heard, pronounce your words clearly so you are understood, and emphasize your ideas with inflection, facial expression, and gesture so that your audience recognizes the important points.

- Give a quality performance.

  Develop ideas with your audience in mind, presenting them in an interesting manner. Always maintain control over the presentation so that your audience does not take over. A quality performance is the result of thorough preparation and dynamic presentation.

PRESENTING YOURSELF

In every speaking situation your attitude toward yourself, your listeners, and your subject significantly affects what you say and how you say it.

Attitude toward Yourself

Each of us carries a picture of ourselves as a person—a self-concept or image of the kind of individual we are and of how others perceive us. We think of ourselves as successful or unsuccessful, as liked or disliked, as competent or incompetent to discuss a given topic or make a given judgment, and as someone whose opinions are respected or discounted.

Our self-image influences how we are likely to behave in a given speaking situation. If a speaker has a low opinion of his or her ability or is unsure about the subject, ideas are presented in a random or confused manner. The voice is weak and unsteady, the body is stiff and restrained, and the eyes are directed toward the floor or ceiling rather than toward the audience. Because of fear, opinions are weakened and as a result stated less strongly than the supporting facts or circumstances warrant (Gronbeck, Ehninger, and Monroe, 1988).

In contrast, if a speaker has exaggerated ideas of his knowledge or abilities, he is more likely to adopt a strong and overbearing manner, to disregard the need for facts and proofs, and to state his ideas without regard for the opinions and feelings of his audience. In both instances, self-image exercises a major, negative influence on the content and the style of the message and determines in advance how ideas will be received.

Attitude toward Listeners

A second important influence on speaking behavior is the attitude toward listeners. Each time we speak, we do so from a certain status or role position: seller or buyer, parent or child, teacher or student, boss or employee, creditor or debtor, doctor or patient, stranger or friend. And as our role positions change, so do our attitudes toward our listeners. As a result, we talk in one way to individuals we know well and in quite a different way to casual acquaintances or strangers (Gronbeck, Ehninger, and Monroe, 1988).

Similarly, our speaking manner changes as we communicate with those who are above or below us in a social or professional hierarchy. The middle-management executive uses a deferential manner when talking to the big bosses, an open and relaxed style when conferring with other middle-management persons, and an authoritative tone when addressing lower management or shop foremen.

Attitude toward Subject

Finally, our behavior as speakers is influenced by how we feel about the subject we are discussing—whether we believe or disbelieve what we are saying, and whether we regard it as interesting or boring, pertinent or irrelevant, crucial or trivial. Our attitude influences the ideas we present and the language in which we express them. And it is reflected in our voice and appearance, factors that also reveal our attitudes toward ourselves and toward our listeners.

THE THREE-STEP PROCESS

When you make a presentation, your goal is to create the desired response from your audience. To get the desired response, follow a three-step process: preassessment, preparation, and delivering the presentation.

Step One: Preassessment (Audience Analysis)

Understanding your audience and their needs will assist you in convincing them of your ideas. Effective presentation depends on more than simply stating your ideas, opinions, or values; it requires that you relate what you have to say to your audience. In each presentation you make you will have a unique audience, even if you are speaking to the same group of people. People change over time, as do their needs, wants, and desires. For each presentation you give, you need to consider the needs, wants, desires, beliefs, and attitudes of the audience you're addressing.

Understanding your audience is the backbone of a successful presentation. Before you begin to plan a presentation, you should know as much as possible about who will be listening to you, their backgrounds, beliefs, and social positions, as well as their knowledge about and involvement with your topic. Moreover, you need to continually assess your audience during the presentation itself. You must note how your audience responds and if necessary adapt or alter your presentation to make it more effective.

It is your responsibility to see that your listeners understand, to respond to the feedback you receive, and to talk with your audience rather than at them. Finally, your goal should be to enhance the audience, not yourself. If the audience will learn nothing or remain unaffected by your presentation, the presentation should not be given. Assessing your audience and the needs of its members gives more impact to your presentation.

Audience Attitudes

It is important to consider the attitudes your audience holds toward your ideas. This factor bears directly on the tactics you should use to make your presentation and on your chances of being effective. Each group of listeners will have some feelings about your ideas before you present them. These feelings can be expressed in one of the following ways: the audience will agree with the ideas; the audience will disagree with them; or the audience will be indifferent (Oliver, 1957).

When preassessing your audience, if you find your audience already endorses what you have to say, your goal is to reinforce the positive attitudes that already exist. The presentation will encourage the audience to maintain or increase their commitment. At times you will face a hostile audience, one that is already opposed to your ideas. Preassessment should ensure that this comes as no surprise. Your task will then be to overcome as much of the listeners' resistance as possible. You can reduce outspoken and private opposition and move your audience toward neutrality or indecision on the issue. You must plan your presentation thoroughly, make arguments from the ground up, acknowledge the opposing point of view, and present your argument as strongly as possible. If your ideas are new or unusual, your audience may not know enough before your presentation to make a sound judgment. To win their support, you need to provide that information. You need to proceed at a pace appropriate to your audience's level of understanding.

Audience Characteristics

Audience characteristics include data about individual personalities, demographic information, the constituencies your audience represents, and the roles of members of the audience. When considered before your presentation, this information helps you to decide how to aim or slant the presentation for maximum effect.

Each audience has its own personality. You will need to gather as much information as possible about both the individual and collective personalities of your audience. Demographics include facts about age, sex, race, religion, nationality, education, political beliefs, social and economic circumstances, and organizational roles. Pay close attention to these elements when planning your presentation and look for what is unusual in your audience to obtain clues about how it may best be approached, informed, or persuaded. You will need to consider the range of roles that your audience plays at various times and, especially, while listening to the presentation. Key factors include who is in your audience and what your presentation is about. If you have top management and production workers in your audience, you will want to consider their reactions to your ideas based upon the roles they play due to their positions and as audience members.

Once you determine who will be present, and gather data about your audience, prepare a preassessment worksheet using the one in Figure 10.1 as a guide. Use the worksheet to describe how you think your audience will react to your presentation. Based on the information in your worksheet, create the basic outline of your presentation. As more information becomes available, review and revise your presentation.

Figure 10.1 Preassessment Worksheet

1. Is this presentation necessary? Why?
2. What do you hope to achieve in giving this presentation?
3. What specifically will you ask your audience to do as a result of your presentation?
4. How do you describe your audience in terms of:

Age	Economic status
Education	Political status
Organizational role	Other influences

5. What are audience members' political and social orientations?
6. Where do they get their information?
7. What constituencies do they serve?
8. What do they think of your proposal?
9. What is the source of their attitudes?
10. What attitudes can be changed?

11. What strategies may work?

12. What do they think of you?

13. What are your strengths (with listeners)?

14. What are your weaknesses (with listeners)?

15. What are your possible sources of credibility?

16. Where and when will the presentation be held?

17. Are there any unusual circumstances surrounding the presentation?

18. Are there any special considerations you should give in planning and delivering your presentation?

Step Two: Preparation

Every business presentation is persuasive. No matter what your topic, you must offer reasons for your listeners to regard what you say as important. Whether you want them to learn something, believe something, or do something, you are obligated to tailor your requests to meet their needs and concerns.

Ineffective speakers offer reasons that make sense only to themselves. Arrogant speakers offer no reasons at all. You must anticipate your listeners' questions and provide answers before they are asked. By concentrating on what is important to your audience, you avoid preoccupation with reasons and justifications that relate only to yourself. The most persuasive presentation is one in which your needs and those of the audience mesh.

The issue is not just to modify your ideas to suit your audience. Rather, you must persuade your audience to modify their ideas to suit you. Changing your ideas merely to win audience approval is dishonest. You have a point to make that you regard as important to the audience. If you can gain the agreement of the audience through the reasons you offer, then you will be successful. The following are some reasons for listening that you can offer your audience (Gronbeck, Ehninger, and Monroe, 1988, p. 76).

1. Your presentation will make their jobs easier.

2. Your presentation will clarify some confusion.

3. Your presentation will mean more money, advancement on the job, security, or employee benefits for them.

4. Your presentation will make their life more pleasant.

5. Your presentation will help them defend themselves against forces that could hurt them.

In addition to offering your audience a good reason to listen, your presentation must be interesting. You can generate interest among those in your audience in some of the following ways:

1. "If you want them to believe what you say, show them how their present beliefs result in unproductive actions, jeopardize their physical and emotional security or confuse them and how your beliefs would benefit them.
2. If you want them to learn something, show them how the effort will be pleasant and will facilitate what they need.
3. If you want them to do something, show them how to do it and how it will help them be safe, use less energy, do better work or find pleasure."

(Phillips, 1982, p. 80)

Normally you would not make a request of an audience unless it is very important and relevant to the situation. People find it uncomfortable to change what they believe or the way they do things, and learning new material takes time and effort. There must be some perceived threat that will result if they do not do what you ask, and some clear benefit if they do. You must first give your listeners reason to doubt by providing arguments that reveal weaknesses in what they know, believe, or do. Then you must show them how the ideas or procedures you propose will make things better.

Stating Goals and Reasons for Listening

The first step in preparing your presentation is to set goals. Your goals statement is about what your audience is to know, believe, or do as a result of your presentation, for example:

1. I want my audience to know that new regulations for reporting accidents will be in place.
2. I want my audience to realize that reducing accidents makes good financial sense.
3. I want my audience to be well informed on how to fill out the new accident report forms.

The second step in preparation is to make some kind of statement that specifies how you will know when you have attained your goal, as in the following examples:

1. I will be successful if some good questions are asked by people in the audience when I have finished my presentation.
2. I will be successful if those in the audience give their own examples of why they believe the idea I have suggested to them.

3. I will be successful if members of the audience do the task correctly.

Your third step is to discover the reasons that your audience will be worse off if they do not accept your idea and helped if they do accept it. Consider the following examples:

1. If they do not fill out the forms correctly, they will not be compensated for their expenses; they will be helped if they are compensated.
2. They could lose their jobs if unsafe behavior continues; they will keep their health and their jobs if they work safely.
3. Further accidents will close down the production line; they will be helped because correct performance could result in increased production schedules and greater profitability.

Organizing Ideas

Why organize your presentation? There are many good reasons.

1. To develop your idea completely.
2. To cover your topic in a specific time frame.
3. To ensure your audience digests the ideas that you present.
4. To help your audience understand that what you say is important.
5. To help your audience remember the important concepts.

The most efficient way to prepare your presentation is to reduce your message to a few sentences. Think of what you would like your audience to remember if they forget 95 percent of what you say. What would you want to remain in their heads? An example follows.

1. Accidents are up 37 percent from this time last year.
2. The lost dollars have put us on the edge of bankruptcy,
3. I want each person present to call in his or her subordinates and explain that starting tomorrow, supervisors will be observing for unsafe behavior on a daily basis.

If those in the audience remember these three things, they may do something that will reduce accidents in the weeks ahead.

Organizing entails breaking your topic into manageable parts. This process makes it easier for you to present the relevant information and for your audience to receive and remember it. Figure 10.2 suggests six steps to follow in organizing your presentation.

Figure 10.2 Steps to Follow in Organizing Your Ideas

1. Decide exactly what you want to say in your presentation.
2. After careful thought, eliminate those things that are not directly related to what you want to say.
3. Make a list of the ideas that are the main points you hope to make in your presentation.
4. Look for information that supports, clarifies, and illustrates your main points.
5. Use the main points that you have selected to build an outline.
6. Be prepared to modify and refine your outline as you do more research and learn additional facts about your intended audience.

Using Supporting Materials

To be taken seriously, you need to build a case to support your topic. Supporting materials are the evidence and documentation that expand the major points in your presentation. Supporting materials strengthen your arguments and encourage the audience to understand and believe what they hear. To support your position you can use personal experience, testimony, analogy, explanations, comparisons, contrasts, illustration, specific instances, and statistics.

Sometimes two or more kinds of supporting materials are combined, as when statistics are used to develop an illustration or when the testimony of an authority is given to strengthen or verify an explanation. At other times these materials are used singly. Your choice of materials depends upon the type of support you need. Comparisons, contrasts, and hypothetical illustrations, for example, can be especially helpful in making ideas clear and vivid. Specific instances, statistics, and testimony work effectively as proof.

Statistics can also show relationships. They emphasize magnitude and describe subclasses or parts. Because statistics reduce masses of information into generalized categories, they are useful both in making clear the nature of a situation and in substantiating your claim. We often use statistics to describe in a relatively short space the scope or seriousness of a problem, helping the audience grasp clearly the dimension of a problem. Statistics can isolate parts of a problem or show those factors caused by a discrete effect. Using statistics is especially helpful when you are treating highly complex subject matter. Finally, statistics often are used to describe a trend across time. Statistical trends indicate where we have been and where we are going.

When using statistics, keep in mind the following cautions:

1. "Translate difficult-to-comprehend numbers into more . . . understandable terms.

2. Don't be afraid to generalize complicated statistics.

3. Use visual materials to clarify complicated statistical trends or summaries.

4. Use statistics objectively. Remember, statistics don't lie, but liars use statistics.

5. Check the validity of statistical evidence by applying the tests of who, why, when, and how.

   Who collected the data?

   Why were the data collected?

   When were the data collected?

   How were the data collected?

6. Make your numbers and statistics clear and meaningful to your listeners.

7. Make sure the statistics are valid and reliable."

(Gronbeck, Ehninger, and Monroe, 1988, pp. 106–108)

Types of Argument

You can persuade your audience by three types of argument: statements that rely on your credibility or trustworthiness, logical appeals, and emotional appeals. While we all think of ourselves as logical people who form thoughtful opinions based on sound reasoning, we respond to many stimuli that are not logical appeals. Mass media provide striking illustrations of emotional appeals at work. Advertisers attempt to sell soap products through appeals to our vanity, insecurity, and so forth.

By combining the three types of arguments, you can create an effective persuasive presentation. Purely logical arguments can be dry and dull. Overly emotional arguments may make your audience feel that they are being manipulated. Combinations are more effective. A good rule of thumb is to structure your presentation so that you impress the audience with your credibility, convince them through your logic, and finally, move them with your emotional appeals.

CREDIBILITY

The research on credibility has expanded dramatically in recent years. Originally there were just a few credibility factors identified by research, including the following traits:

- Competence. Knowledge of the field.
- Character. Honesty, dependability, trustworthiness.
- Goodwill. Respect for the audience's best interests.

More recent research has added factors as follows:

- Composure. Emotional control of the situation.
- Sociability. Friendliness.
- Extroversion. Outgoing, active, talkative characteristics.
- Dynamism. Enthusiasm.
- Consistency.
- Physical attractiveness.

Credibility is not something you possess; it is something the audience perceives in you and attaches to you and what you say. Further evidence about you or the discovery that the information you present is false will drastically alter the entire perception of your audience. Because the perception is in the audience, you can only behave in a manner that induces the perception of credibility. In other words, make the best impression possible, and you will go a long way in making the information you present credible to your audience.

Use the following guidelines to enhance your credibility when giving a management presentation:

1. Introduce yourself. Tell why you are speaking on the subject and state your expertise. Cite your qualifications without bragging. Establish your credentials. Provide such information in the introduction of your presentation.

2. Have someone introduce you to the audience. Give the person your credentials and have him or her state them for the audience before you speak.

3. Maintain a competent and relaxed delivery. Even the most qualified speaker will appear less credible with a nervous or tense delivery.

4. Limit digressions. You will have more credibility if you are in control of the presentation and tactfully keep on track. Take the situation seriously.

5. Be prepared. If you to "wing it," you will appear less credible to the audience, because it will look as though you do not care about the topic or the listeners. Be prepared for questions and objections.

6. Sound authoritative. Don't talk down to your audience, but do speak confidently. Make sure your posture conveys confidence as well.

7. No one can know everything about a topic area, so don't profess to.

8. Be involved. You need to communicate nonverbally how important the subject is to you. If you don't believe in the topic, why should your audience?

9. Look your best and dress appropriately for the day and place.

10. Show your concern for the audience's best interests.

CREATING TENSION

Sometimes you can persuade your audience by generating tension about their current beliefs. Most people have a need to maintain a condition of internal balance. In other words, we prefer things to be in their place. If faced with either of two incompatible beliefs or with a new fact that is inconsistent with what we already believe, we become uncomfortable. This discomfort produces a state of psychological tension or imbalance. To resolve this tension, we need to restore our sense of balance, which involves a change in attitude or behavior. In other words, creating tension can produce the desired change (Festinger, 1957).

We react to this tension in a variety of ways. We can discount the source of the tension ("He doesn't know what he's talking about anyway"). We can abandon our original opinion ("I didn't really believe that"). We can refuse to deal with the situation ("Don't bother me with that stuff"). We can play down its importance ("It really doesn't matter to me one way or another"). To create tension, say something surprising that upsets your audience's sense of balance. Then offer a vehicle through which your listeners could regain the balance lost in the jolt caused by your initial argument. Their remedy should be to accept your proposal.

Fear appeals create tension as well. Using a strong fear appeal may create attitude change. The person receiving the strong fear appeal may very well discredit the source, refuse to deal with the situation, or play down its importance. Many studies on the use of fear appeals in campaigns have produced results showing that fear appeals do affect performance, while other studies have produced results in the opposite direction (Villardo, 1968). To determine whether a fear appeal will be effective, you need information about your audience, the information they already have, and the length of time after receiving your message that they have to engage in the recommended activity. The more information your audience already has concerning the desired behavior, the more effective the fear appeal will be. If the message recipient does not have the opportunity to immediately engage in the recommended procedure but must retain the message for some period of time, an approach that does not provoke fear will likely have better results.

One such example of fear appeals has been cited by the National Safety Council. The council found that the posters that proved most effective in promoting safe behavior were posters that coupled high threat content with a realistic presentation and a specific message. A study of United Airlines at Chicago's O'Hare International Airport proved that there is a strong correlation between level of threat in safety posters and safe behavior (Piccolino, 1966).

By making your proposal concur with what your audience already believes, you reinforce what is already inside the listeners' minds. Reinforcement works only when your opinions and those of your audience are already closely allied. Reinforcement is the easiest technique because it does not force your listeners to stretch their beliefs, attitudes, wants, or opinions very far. It is successful only when what you have to propose is consistent with what your listeners already want or accept.

Structuring the Presentation for Motivation

By using the five-step process known as Monroe's motivated sequence, you can be more successful in motivating your audience to change their attitudes or take the action you propose (Gronbeck, Ehninger, and Monroe, 1988, p. 273).

1. Attention Step: Draw audience's attention to a particular need and give them a reason to listen.
   Desired Response: "There's something in this for me."
2. Need Step: Challenge the audience with the situation that demands action.
   Desired Response: "We have to do something about this."
3. Satisfaction Step: Propose an action plan to meet the challenge, using facts and and emotional appeals.
   Desired Response: "I want to make this work."
4. Visualization Step: Project in vivid detail the results that such action or the failure to take action will bring.
   Desired Response: "I can see how this will help."
5. Action Step: Request that the audience use the action plan.
   Desired Response: "I'll take the next step today."

Parts of a Presentation

At this point you have developed the body of your presentation. All presentations consist of an introduction, body, and conclusion. Many of us have heard the old adage "Tell them what you're going to tell them, tell them, and tell them what you told them." In preparing a presentation, always start with the body first and then develop an introduction and conclusion.

GETTING ATTENTION: ICEBREAKERS AND INTRODUCTIONS

An effective introduction sets the stage for your presentation. It should include what you intend to talk about and why you have chosen your topic. Indicate specific points you intend to cover in the order in which they will occur in the body of the presentation. This procedure prepares listeners for what you are going to say. Of course, your main presentation should reinforce and expand what you have alluded to in your introduction. You should also build rapport between you and your audience. There are three ways you can develop rapport with your audience: through humor, especially humor directed at yourself; by identifying areas of common interest between you and your audience; and by stressing concern for your audience's welfare.

While the words you choose and the way you organize your presentation reflect your knowledge about the topic, your audience will still want to know why they should believe what you are about to tell them. They need to know what credentials will make your opinion or knowledge of the subject more valuable than that of someone else.

A good introduction personalizes your presentation to make your audience sympathetic and interested in your presentation. One of the best ways to personalize your topic is to ask rhetorical questions. Lively questions arouse your audience's interest and make listeners feel that your topic is important to them.

When giving a presentation, your exposure to your audience is relatively short, and everything you say and do is going to be judged. The first impression you make is the most vital one. The presentation begins the minute you enter the room. The initial impression you make will carry with you throughout the rest of your presentation. With a first impression, your audience judges much of what is to follow. If you make an unfavorable impression in the introduction, your listeners may tune out much of what you want them to hear and respond to. There are several points to keep in mind.

1. Plan, prepare, and rehearse. Consider each phrase and gesture that you will use in front of your audience.
2. Think about your audience. You will want to meet audience expectations about your introduction.
3. Be yourself. Avoid the tendency to be cute or clever unless this is part of the planned introduction and is consistent with your audience's expectation of you.

The chief function of the introduction is to make your audience pay attention to your presentation. There are as many ways of gaining listener attention as there are situations that call for presentations. Some techniques you can use to make sure that your audience tunes into your presentation follow.

- Make a surprising statement at the beginning of your presentation.
- Show a visual or graphic that highlights an important aspect of your presentation.

- Do something interesting physically that is consistent with the purpose of your presentation.
- Quote a famous expert on your topic.
- Refer to something unusual about your audience.
- Pay a special compliment to your audience.

Finally, the introduction allows you to make a smooth transition into the first main point in the body of your presentation. This lead-in should alert your audience to what is to follow and make the progression from one part of the presentation to the next easy to follow.

USING HUMOR

Humor is a powerful tool, but it's tricky to use. An infusion of humor into any presentation can break tension, win over opponents, enhance your image, and make points memorable. You need not consider yourself a humorous speaker or your presentation a humorous talk to benefit from this attention-getter. Developing your use of humor is not a matter of collecting jokes and gags, which have limited usefulness. What is important is the ability to spot a potentially humorous idea in your presentation and to develop it into a genuinely funny moment.

When using humor, use the following guidelines (Sprague and Stewart, 1984, pp. 205–207):

- Avoid humor that may offend your audience.
- Avoid irrelevant humor.
- Do not tell jokes unless you have mastered the techniques of joke telling.
- Do not overintroduce any humorous material.
- Avoid overused material.

CONCLUSIONS

Once you've told them what you're going to tell them (introduction), and told them (body), you should tell them what you've told them (conclusion). The conclusion rounds out your presentation by tying up any loose ends that may be left from the points discussed in the body. It completes the purpose of your talk, and it lets your listeners know that your presentation is about to end. Your conclusion should emphasize the main idea, so that it will be firmly etched in your listeners' memories. Often the conclusion is the most dramatic part of the presentation.

In the conclusion, you only want to remind the listener of the most important points in your presentation. The review leaves your listeners with what you most want them to remember. You should also stress your strongest argument. In addition, effective conclusions ask for some kind of action from the listeners. The conclusion is the place to jolt the audience into acting, using emotional appeals.

The ultimate function of the conclusion is to indicate that your presentation is over. Your conclusion should make this immediately clear. You should also make the conclusion as graceful as possible by not being excessively wordy or redundant. Never end a presentation with "That's about it" or "That's all I wanted to say." Have a final statement and end with a sense of finality.

Step Three: Delivering the Presentation

The final step—delivering the presentation—may be easy for you or have you a bit unnerved. If the latter case is true, you are in good company. A consulting firm asked 2,543 adults to rank order their fears. The following list gives the results of the survey (Wallenchinsky, 1978, p. 469).

1. Speaking before a group
2. Fear of heights
3. Insects and bugs
4. Financial problems
5. Deep water
6. Sickness
7. Death
8. Flying
9. Loneliness
10. Dogs

As you can see, speaking before a group is ranked even higher than the fear of death. So if you experience a sense of fear or anxiety about giving a presentation, you are quite normal.

Communication Apprehension

Communication apprehension is the communication scientist's term for stage fright or speech anxiety. It is a temporary state of fear caused by the anticipation of participation in a presentation to a group of people. It is normal, healthy, and universal.

Why does this phenomenon occur? Communication apprehension occurs because our ego and self-esteem are threatened. When we feel threatened either physically or psychologically, our body responds with a chemical reaction and adrenaline begins to flow. This chemical reaction can be brought on by either actual or anticipated danger (McCrosky, 1979).

Figure 10.3 lists some common symptoms of communication apprehension. You may find some of them familiar.

Figure 10.3 Symptoms of Communication Apprehension

1. Frog in the throat
2. Hands held tight in front or back of the body
3. Clutching the lectern or podium as if under attack
4. Scratching face or arms
5. Raised voice level
6. Red blotches on neck and chest
7. Sweaty palms

Let's look closer at the chemical reaction that takes place. Adrenaline flowing through the bloodstream causes a number of reactions.

1. The senses become more acute and alert.
2. Blood leaves the stomach and moves to larger muscle groups (often causing "butterflies" in the stomach).
3. Breathing is faster and shallower (often causing hyperventilation).
4. Larger muscle groups in extremities become very tense. Muscles may become tired or shaky.
5. Blood in extremities causes them become warm, resulting in perspiration to cool the body.
6. The digestive system is given low priority. The salivary glands limit their secretion, resulting in a dry mouth.

As you look at these symptoms and bodily reactions, you might notice that nearly all of them are invisible to your audience. It helps to remember that probably the only one who knows you're nervous is you.

Remember that it is normal to be nervous before giving a presentation. It is important to channel that nervous energy and make the adrenaline work for you rather than seemingly against you. The following suggestions will help you give more polished presentations while keeping anxiety to a minimum.

1. Speak often. The more you speak in front of groups, the less likely you are to feel anxious. You might even find yourself looking forward to the occasions.
2. Prepare thoroughly. By preparing thoroughly, you will automatically feel more confident in your presentation. You can also ensure that you then know your topic better than anyone.

3. Practice aloud. If at all possible, practice your presentation ten times. Do it in front of a mirror, a spouse, coworkers, or a video camera. Seek feedback and practice expressing yourself in a variety of ways, covering the same material. This process will allow you to speak freely with minimal use of notes.

4. Focus on your audience rather than yourself. If you are thinking about how you sound or look or wondering what the audience thinks of your presentation, you're less likely to succeed. Focus on the audience. Are they listening, interested, bored? Do you need to take a break, tell a story, or wrap up the presentation? For an effective presentation, remember to be receiver-centered.

5. Use your voice and body to your advantage. Channel any nervous energy. Take a brisk walk before the presentation and use gestures and varied pitch and rate of speech while making the presentation. Feel free to walk around as you speak; walking engages the audience and holds their interest.

6. Keep in mind that no one knows you're nervous but you.

7. Look your best and dress appropriately.

Figure 10.4 provides a personal report of communication apprehension.

**Figure 10.4 Personal Report of Communication
            Apprehension (PRCA)**

Directions: This instrument is composed of twenty-five statements concerning feelings about communicating with other people. Please indicate the degree to which each statement applies to you by marking whether you (1) strongly agree, (2) agree, (3) are undecided, (4) disagree, or (5) strongly disagree with each statement. There are no right or wrong answers. Work quickly; just record your first impression.

1. While participating in a conversation with a new acquaintance I feel very nervous. 1 2 3 4 5
2. I have no fear of facing an audience. 1 2 3 4 5
3. I talk less because I'm shy. 1 2 3 4 5
4. I look forward to expressing my opinions at meetings. 1 2 3 4 5
5. I am afraid to express myself in a group. 1 2 3 4 5
6. I look forward to an opportunity to speak in public. 1 2 3 4 5

7. I find the prospect of speaking mildly pleasant.	1	2	3	4	5
8. When communicating, my posture feels strained and unnatural.	1	2	3	4	5
9. I am tense and nervous while participating in group discussion.	1	2	3	4	5
10. Although I talk fluently with friends, I am at a loss for words on the platform.	1	2	3	4	5
11. I have no fear about expressing myself in a group.	1	2	3	4	5
12. My hands tremble when I try to handle objects on the platform.	1	2	3	4	5
13. I always avoid speaking in public if possible.	1	2	3	4	5
14. I feel that I am more fluent when talking to people than most other people are.	1	2	3	4	5
15. I am fearful and tense all the while I am speaking before a group of people.	1	2	3	4	5
16. My thoughts become confused and jumbled when I speak before an audience.	1	2	3	4	5
17. I like to get involved in group discussions.	1	2	3	4	5
18. Although I am nervous just before getting up, I soon forget my fears and enjoy the experience.	1	2	3	4	5
19. Conversing with people who hold positions of authority causes me to be fearful and tense.	1	2	3	4	5
20. I dislike using my body and voice expressively.	1	2	3	4	5
21. I feel relaxed and comfortable while speaking.	1	2	3	4	5
22. I feel self-conscious when I am called upon to answer a question or give an opinion in class.	1	2	3	4	5

23. I face the prospect of making a speech with complete confidence.	1	2	3	4	5
24. I'm afraid to speak up in conversations.	1	2	3	4	5
25. I would enjoy presenting a speech on a local television show.	1	2	3	4	5

Scoring the PRCA

To compute your PRCA score, follow these three steps:

1) Add your score for items 1, 3, 5, 8, 9, 10, 12, 13, 15, 16, 19, 20, 22, and 24.
2) Add up your scores for items 2, 4, 6, 7, 11, 14, 17, 18, 21, 23, and 25.
3) Complete the following formula:

PRCA score = 84 − (total from step 1) + (total from step 2).

The Personal Report of Communication Apprehension (PRCA) is an instrument that measures your motivation toward verbal communication. The PRCA has been used extensively in a variety of studies and environments, and all reports suggest that the PRCA is both a highly reliable and a valid measure of an individual's level of apprehension about oral communication.

If you score 75 or above on the PRCA, this is an indication that you have some communication apprehension. If you score an 88 or above, this indicates that you are a high communication apprehensive.

Source: James C. McCrosky, West Virginia University.

Methods and Elements of Delivery

Choosing the best method of delivery will help make your presentation effective. You need to consider type of delivery as well as visual and vocal elements, which include your choice of words, how you look, and how you sound.

There are four types of delivery from which to choose, as follows:

1. Impromptu. Impromptu speaking is done with very little preparation—only a few moments' thought. If you are not an expert in the subject area, choosing this type of delivery is not a good idea. Impromptu presentation often can come across as poorly prepared, thereby reducing the speaker's credibility. Choose an impromptu delivery only if you are an expert and an "off the top of my head" style is appropriate to the occasion.

2. Read from a manuscript. This type of delivery is seldom appropriate for a management presentation. It is an automatic audience turnoff. While you may need notes from which to speak, avoid reading your presentation.

3. Memorized. You may choose to memorize all of your presentation or just the introduction, in order to start in a bold and self-assured manner. The main drawback to memorizing a presentation is that each thought hinges upon the previous idea. When memory blocks occur, and they will, the remainder of the material is lost as well. Try to avoid memorizing the entire presentation, but you can certainly commit the introduction to memory.

4. Extemporaneous. This type of delivery is neither read nor memorized. It is based on thorough preparation and practice, and utilizes a minimum of notes. By rehearsing the presentation, you will begin to find it easy to present your ideas differently each time, giving you more flexibility and the appearance of being spontaneous.

VISUAL ELEMENTS

Appearance is an important part of a good delivery. You can improve your visual effectiveness by using the following guidelines (Adler, 1986, pp. 320–323).

1. Dress appropriately. If the occasion calls for casual attire, a formal appearance can be just as harmful as underdressing. While appearance is always important, it is even more so when you get up to give your latest proposal to top management. As a general rule of thumb, determine audience attire and then wear something that is just a bit more formal. One can always remove a coat or a tie. This shows the audience that you are serious, yet you're someone they can identify with.

2. Speak with confidence and authority. Speakers who fidget while waiting to speak, clutch the podium as if they were facing a firing squad, and then fumble with their notes send the nonverbal message "I'm not sure about myself or what I have to say." An audience will discount even the best ideas when they're delivered with such a powerful nonverbal message.

3. Get set before speaking. If you need an easel or overhead projector, move it into position before you begin. If needed, adjust the microphone, close the door, reset the air conditioner, or rearrange the seating. Position yourself physically before beginning. Sometimes, out of nervousness, a speaker will blurt out opening remarks before he or she is set to speak. It is better to stand or walk to the

position from which you will talk, get set, wait a brief moment, and then begin speaking.

4. Establish and maintain eye contact. If you talk directly to the audience, you will be seen as more involved and sincere. Use the moment before you speak to look around the room. Let the audience know by your glance that you are interested in them. Be sure your glance covers virtually everyone in the room or, if the group is too large, choose a few people in different parts of the room, making eye contact with each one for a few seconds.

5. Begin without looking at your notes. Make contact with the audience as you begin speaking. You can't do this if you are looking at your notes. This means you will want to have your introduction down pat.

6. Speak with enthusiasm. If you don't appear to be excited about the importance of your subject, there's little chance that the audience will. Think of your presentation as sharing ideas you truly believe in. Often, the stress of giving the presentation causes you to forget how important your remarks are. Remind yourself why you are speaking during the moments before you speak.

7. Stand and move with a purpose. Stand in a relaxed but firm manner. Place your feet firmly on the ground, spaced apart the distance of your shoulder width. Hold your head upright, turning naturally to look at the audience. Moving about can add life to your presentation and help release nervous energy as well as hold attention. Your actions should always be purposeful. Nervous pacing might help the speaker feel better, but it may distract the audience.

8. Don't emphasize mistakes. Even the best speakers forget or bungle a line occasionally. The difference between professionals and amateurs is in the way they handle such mistakes. Experts simply go on, adjusting their remarks to make the error less noticeable.

9. Don't pack up early. Gathering your notes or starting for your chair before concluding is a nonverbal statement that you're anxious to get the presentation finished. Even if you are, making it obvious will cause your audience to feel that your presentation is less valuable.

10. Move with confidence when finished. When you end your remarks or finish answering questions, leave your place confidently. Most speakers are their own best critics. Even if you are disappointed with your delivery, don't let the audience see that. You're probably overly critical of yourself. Usually the audience will rate you more favorably than you would.

VOCAL ELEMENTS

Your voice can communicate your attitude about yourself, your topic, and your audience. It can also send signals about your enthusiasm or disinterest, confidence or nervousness, friendliness or hostility, and respect or disdain. The following are some guidelines for good vocal delivery.

1. Speak loudly enough to be heard. Listeners often interpret an overly soft voice as a sign of timidity or lack of conviction.
2. Avoid "ums" and "uhs." A few will go unnoticed, but more than that can be distracting. Simply paying attention to the times you use them will put them to rest. Instead of inserting syllables when you are thinking of what to say next, just take a brief pause.

See Figure 10.5 for a checklist for the most important elements of effective delivery.

Figure 10.5 Checklist for Effective Delivery:
Visual and Vocal Elements

Visual Elements

Dress appropriately.
Step up to speak with confidence and authority.
Get set before speaking.
Establish and maintain eye contact.
Begin without looking at notes.
Speak extemporaneously, with enthusiasm and sincerity.
Stand and move effectively.
Don't emphasize mistakes.
Don't pack up early.
Leave your place smartly when finished.

Vocal Elements

Speak loudly enough to be heard.
Speak without excessive "ums" and "uhs."
Use proper vocabulary and pronunciation.
Enunciate clearly.

Using Visual Aids Effectively

All visual aids should work to enhance audience interest in your presentation. They should be part of the gradual buildup to your presentation's climax. For this reason, timing is very important. In most instances it is best to conceal a visual aid until the exact moment it is needed.

One of the worst things you can do is to present your aids ineffectively. This includes not knowing how to run equipment like projectors and tape recorders. Your visual aid should be ready to be used when your presentation calls for it. Before the presentation, set up the visual and then check the back of the room to see how it will look to your audience. Sit in different seats and notice how the view changes from each. When speaking, be sure not to block the aid from your audience. When referring to your aid, talk to your audience, not to the aid. Stand to one side and point to the visual. When you are finished with the aid, remove it from view. Leaving it in place can be distracting and can take attention away from you.

Graphs, charts, or diagrams should be drawn as simply and clearly as possible. Bright, distinct colors help to distinguish different objects. Overlapping transparencies are useful for explaining relationships between different objects on the graph, diagram, or chart. Consider room size and acoustics. Use the guidelines in Figure 10.6 to determine if your presentation needs a visual aid.

Figure 10.6 Is a Visual Aid Necessary?

1. Does the visual aid improve communication with your audience?
2. Are you familiar with how to use it?
3. Will it provide the audience with new information?
4. Can the aid be handled appropriately in the presentation environment?
5. Will the aid dominate your presentation?
6. Will the aid stimulate audience interest?
7. Does the aid enhance your credibility?
8. Does the aid reinforce a key concept of your presentation?

QUESTION-AND-ANSWER SESSIONS

While a written report might leave readers confused or unimpressed, your on-the-spot response to questions and concerns can win over an audience.

When to Answer Questions

Whenever possible, you should control the timing of audience questions.

1. During the presentation. This approach allows you to address the audience's concerns immediately. However, it does have its drawbacks. Some questions are premature. Others are irrelevant and may waste time. If you choose to handle questions during your presentation, allow for extra time and promise to answer premature questions later in your presentation.

2. After the presentation. This approach allows you to control the way your information is reviewed. You also have more control over the length of your presentation. However, when you deny listeners the chance to speak up and ask questions, they may be so preoccupied with questions or concerns that they miss most of what you say. If you choose this method, use the following guidelines:

- Acknowledge the questions your audience has and promise to answer them later in a question-and-answer period.
- Save time for a brief summary after the question-and-answer period.

How to Manage Questions

1. You can get the question-and-answer session rolling with your own remarks if your audience is hesitant. For example, you can say, "One question you may be asking yourself is. . . ."
2. Anticipate possible questions. Put yourself in your audience's position. Try to prepare responses to their possible inquiries.
3. Clarify complicated questions. Make sure you understand the question by rephrasing it in your own words, starting with "If I understand your question, you're asking. . . ." This response helps you understand the query and gives you a few moments to frame an answer.
4. Take every question seriously. You can even compliment the person asking an interesting question.
5. Don't let questions draw you off track. Try to frame answers while promoting your objective. You can avoid offensive questions by promising to discuss the matter with the questioner in detail after the session or send the person information in follow-up correspondence.
6. If you need a few moments to plan an answer to a surprise question, you can buy time in several ways. You can rephrase the question or ask the person who has the question to do so. You can turn the question around with "How would you address this situation if you were answering?" or "I'd like to know your position on that matter; what do you think?"

AUDIENCE TURNOFFS

Keep your audience in mind, and try to avoid the following audience turnoffs.

Appearing unprepared

Improper handling of questions

Apologizing for yourself or your organization

Being unfamiliar with knowable information (names, companies, latest issues, etc.)

Unprofessional use of audiovisual aids

Seeming to be off schedule

Not establishing personal rapport and empathy

Appearing disorganized

Not starting off quickly in order to establish a strong and positive image

Being theoretical rather than practical

Being negative

ROOM SETUP

Whenever possible, visit your speaking location ahead of time. Note equipment you will need and items to be moved and make the necessary arrangements. Ideally, you want to find an area of the room where distractions are minimized. For example, if you are opposite from the door, your audience is less likely to be distracted by people who need to leave the room during your presentation.

To encourage interaction and less formality, arrange tables or chairs such that they are at angles to your platform, podium, or table. Also, consider the audience's view and arrange seating so that you and your visual aids will be easy to see. If you are sitting at a table, speak from the head of the table and stand when you speak. Your voice travels and projects better when you stand.

Arrive early at your speaking location on the day of your presentation. Make sure room temperature and lighting are satisfactory for the audience size. Make sure all equipment is in proper working order, and if not, make the necessary arrangements before the audience members arrive. Furthermore, being there early suggests to the audience that you care and are interested and well prepared.

Using an Overhead Projector

When you use an overhead projector and transparencies, keep the following in mind:

- Keep the room fully lit for greater group attention and participation.
- Read from the projector, facing the participants (rather than the screen), for better control and for picking up and responding to participant reactions immediately.
- Whenever you want to make a verbal point or shift the participants' attention back to you, *turn off the projector*. All eyes will automatically turn to you.
- When you want to reveal material point by point, use your pen or pencil to point to the item on the transparency—not the screen. If you want to discuss the item, simply lay the pen or pencil on the transparency with the point directed at the item.
- Always have an extra felt-tip pen, an extension cord, and extra light bulbs, just in case. One never knows when they might be needed.

See Figure 10.7 for a checklist that can help you ensure that every presentation is one that makes a difference.

Figure 10.7 Checklist for Presentations

1. What do you want to achieve in the presentation?
2. What will you ask your audience to do as a result of your presentation?
3. What are the audience demographics?
4. What are the audience's attitudes toward your presentation?
5. What are the audience's attitudes toward you?
6. What can you do to increase your credibility?
7. Can you offer the audience a good reason to listen to your presentation?
8. What are your goals for giving the presentation?
9. How will you know when you have attained your goal?
10. How will the audience be affected if they do not accept your idea?
11. How will the audience be affected if they do accept your idea?
12. Have you organized your idea into a single memorable statement?
13. Which motivating techniques do you plan to use?
14. What supporting materials will you be using?
15. Have you developed your introduction and conclusion?
16. How will you coordinate your nonverbal and verbal messages so that they match?
17. How will you manage your appearance, vocal quality, space, and time?
18. How will you use humor?
19. How will you channel your presentation anxiety?

References ▲

Adams, James Stacey, "Towards an Understanding of Inequity," *Journal of Abnormal and Social Psychology*, 1963.

Adams, John P., *Understanding and Managing Stress: A Book of Readings*, San Diego, California, University Associates, 1980.

Adler, Ronald B., *Communicating at Work*, New York, McGraw-Hill, 1983, 1986, 1989.

Argyris, Chris, *Interpersonal Competence and Organizational Effectiveness*, Homewood, Illinois, Irwin-Dorsey, 1962.

Atkinson, J. W., and McClelland, D. C., *A Theory of Achievement Motivation*, New York, Wiley, 1966.

Becker, S. L., and Eckdom, L. R. V., "That Forgotten Basic Skill: Oral Communication," *Association for Communication Administration Bulletin* 33, 1980.

Berlew, David E., and Hall, Douglas T., "The Socialization of Managers: Effects of Expectations on Performance," *Administrative Science Quarterly*, September 1966.

Berne, Eric, *Games People Play*, New York, Random House, 1964.

Blanchard, Kenneth, and Johnson, Spencer, *The One-Minute Manager*, New York, Berkley Books, 1982.

Bowman, G. W. , "What Helps or Harms Promotability?" *Harvard Business Review* 42, January/February 1964.

Burke, Ronald J., and Wilcox, Douglas S., "Characteristics of Effective Performance Appraisal Reviews and Developmental Reviews," *Personnel Psychology* 22, 1969.

Coleman, D., "The Electronic Rorschach," *Psychology Today*, February 1983.

DiSalvo, V., Larsen, D. C., and Seiler, W. J., "Communication Skills Needed by Persons in Business Organizations," College Placement Council, *Communication Education* 25, 1976.

Dover, C., "Listening—The Missing Link in Communication," *General Electric Review* 61, no. 3, May 1958.

Downs, Cal W., Berg, D. M., and Linkugel, W. A., *The Organizational Communicator*, New York, Harper and Row, 1980.

Endicott, Frank S., "The Endicott Report: Trends in the Employment of College and University Graduates in Business and Industry," Northwestern University, Evanston, Illinois, 1980.

Festinger, Leon, *A Theory of Cognitive Dissonance*, Evanston, Illinois, Row Peterson, 1957.

Filey, Alan C., *Interpersonal Conflict Resolution*, National Training Laboratories, Glenview, Illinois, Scott, Foresman, 1975.

Foster, et al., "A Market Study for the College of Business Administration,"unpublished survey, University of Minnesota, Twin Cities, Minneapolis, Minnesota, 1978.

Goetzinger, Charles, "An Analysis of Irritating Factors in Initial Employment Interviews of College Graduates," unpublished Doctoral Dissertation, Purdue University, 1954.

Goldhaber, Gerald, *Organizational Communication*, Dubuque, Iowa, William C. Brown, 1979.

Gronbeck, Bruce, Ehninger, Douglas, and Monroe, Alan, *Principles of Speech Communication*, Glenview, Illinois, Scott, Foresman, 1988.

Hart, Roderick P., and Burks, Don M., "Rhetorical Sensitivity and Social Interaction," *Speech Monographs*, Vol. 39, Speech Communication Association, Annandale, Virginia, June 1972.

Hart, Roderick P., Carlson, Robert E., and Eadie, William F., "Attitudes toward Communication and the Assessment of Rhetorical Sensitivity,"*Communication Monographs*, Vol. 47, Speech Communication Association, Annandale, Virginia, Mar. 1980.

Harvey, O. J., "Beliefs and Behavior: Some Implications for Education," *The Science Teacher*, Dec. 1970.

Herzberg, Frederick, *The Motivation to Work*, New York, Wiley, 1959.

Hunt, Gary T., *Public Speaking*, Englewood Cliffs, New Jersey, Prentice Hall, 1987.

"Instruction in Communication at Colorado State University, College of Engineering," unpublished survey, Colorado State University, Ft. Collins, Colorado, 1979.

Janis, Irving L., *Victims of Groupthink*, Boston, Houghton Mifflin, 1972.

Kerr, Steven, "On the Folly of Rewarding A, While Hoping for B," *Readings in Interpersonal and Organizational Communication*, ed. Huseman, Richard, Logue, Cal, and Freshley, Dwight, Boston, Holbrook Press, 1977.

Kilmann, Ralph H., and Thomas, Kenneth W., "Interpersonal Conflict Handling Behavior as Reflections of Jungian Personality Dimensions," *Psychological Reports* 37, 1975.

Koehler, J. W., and Huber, *Organizational Communication*, 1976.

Kotter, J. P., "What Effective Managers Really Do," *Harvard Business Review* 60, November/December 1982.

Leary, Timothy, *Interpersonal Diagnosis of Personality*, New York, Ronald, 1957.

Lederer, W. J., and Jackson, D., *Mirages of Marriage*, New York, Norton, 1968.

Likert, Rensis, *New Patterns of Management*, New York, McGraw-Hill, 1976.

Livingston, J. Sterling, "Pygmalion in Management," *Harvard Business Review*, 1969.

Luft, Joseph, and Ingham, Harry, *Of Human Interaction*, Palo Alto, California, National Press Books, 1969.

Mayfield, H., "In Defense of Performance Appraisals," *Harvard Business Review* 37, January/February 1980.

McCrosky, James C., "The Impact of Communication Apprehension on Individuals in Organizations," *Communication Quarterly* 27, 1979.

McBrearty, James, *The Art of Job Hunting*, 1972.

McLuhan, Marshall, *Understanding Media: The Extensions of Man*, New York, McGraw-Hill, 1964.

Mehrabian, Albert, and Weiner, M., "Recording of Inconsistent Communications," *Journal of Personality and Social Psychology* 6, 1967.

Meyer, Herbert E., "The Science of Telling Executives How They're Doing," *Fortune*, January 1974.

Meyers, M. Scott, "Conditions for Manager Motivation," *Harvard Business Review*, January/February 1966.

Muchinsky, P., "Performance Ratings of Engineers: Do Graduates Fit the Bill?" *Engineering Education*, November 1974.

Myers, Gail, and Myers, Michelle Tolela, *The Dynamics of Human Communication: A Lab Approach*, New York, McGraw-Hill, 1985.

Nichols, Ralph, and Stevens, Leonard, *Are You Listening?* New York, McGraw-Hill, 1957.

Nunally, Elam, Miller, Sherod, and Wackman, Daniel, *Alive and Aware, Improving Communication in Relationships*, Littleton, Colorado, Interpersonal Communication Programs, 1975.

Oliver, Robert T., *The Psychology of Persuasive Speech*, New York, Longmans Green, 1957.

Olson, Susan, "The Relationship between Rhetorical Sensitivity and Managerial Success," doctoral dissertation, University of Arizona, Tucson, Arizona, 1985.

Pashaliah and Crissy, "The Interview: The Reliability and Validity of the Assessment Interview as a Screening and Selection Technique in the Submarine Service," *MLR Report*, vol. 216, XII, no. 1, Jan. 1953.

Peters, Thomas J., and Waterman, R. H., *In Search of Excellence: Lessons from America's Best-Run Companies*, New York, Harper and Row, 1982.

Phillips, Gerald M., *Communicating in Organizations*, New York, MacMillan, 1982.

Piccolino, E. B., "Depicted Threat Realism and Specificity: Variables Governing Safety Poster Effectiveness," *National Safety News*, June 1969.

Rosenthal, Robert, *Pygmalion in the Classroom*, New York, Holt, Rinehart and Winston, 1968.

Rossiter, Charles, and Pearce, Barnett, *Communicating Personally*, Indianapolis, Bobbs Merrill, 1975.

Satir, Virginia, *Peoplemaking*, Palo Alto, California, Science and Behavior Books, 1972.

Skinner, B. F., *Contingencies of Reinforcement*, New York, Appleton-Century Crofts, 1969.

Sloan, A. P., "Some Determinants of Early Managerial Success," *Sloan Management Review*, 1964.

Spingbett, B. M., "Factors Affecting the Final Decision in the Employment Interview," *Canadian Journal of Psychology* XII, 1958.

Sprague, Jo, and Stewart, Douglas, *The Speaker's Handbook*, Orlando, Florida, Harcourt Brace Jovanovich, 1984.

Srivastva, Suresh, *The Executive Mind*, San Francisco, California, Jossey-Bass Management Series and Science and Behavior Books, 1983.

Steil, Lyman, Barker, Larry, and Watson, Kittie, *Effective Listening: Keys to Your Success*, Reading, Massachusetts, Addison-Wesley, 1983.

Stewart, Charles J., and Cash, William B., Jr., *Interviewing: Principles and Practices*, Dubuqe, Iowa, William C. Brown, 1985.

Swingle, Paul, *Dangerous Games: The Structure of Conflict*, New York, Academy Press, 1970.

Szilagy, Andrew, and Wallace, Mark, *Managing Behavior in Organizations: Organizational Behavior and Performance*, Santa Monica, California, Goodyear, 1982.

Thornton, Don E., "Want the Job? Ask for It," *Tucson Employer*, November 1989.

Tschirgi, H. D., "What Do Recruiters Really Look for in a Candidate?" *Journal of College Placement*, December/January 1973.

Villardo, Frank J., "Review of the Literature on Safety Posters: Why, How, When to Use Fear," paper read at National Safety Council meeting, 1968.

Wallenchinsky, David, *The Book of Lists*, New York, Bantam, 1978.

Wilmot, Joyce, and Wilmot, William, *Interpersonal Conflict*, Dubuque, Iowa, William C. Brown, 1978.

Wyllie, J. D., "Oral Communications: Surveys and Suggestions," *American Business Communication Association Bulletin*, June 1980.

Zima, Joseph, *Interviewing: Key to Effective Management*, Chicago, Science Research Associates, 1983.

Index

achievement 57
Adams, J. 32, 75, 76, 120
Adler, R. 47, 111, 174
agenda 139, 140
appraisal interview 105–111
Argyris, C. 31
assumptions 4, 8, 9, 32
Atkinson, J. 57
audience turn-offs 178–179

Becker, S. and Eckdom, L. 44
Berlew, D. and Hall, D. 55, 56
Blanchard, K. and Johnnson, S. 81
Bowman, G. 6, 42
Burke, R. and Wilcox, D. 107

calibrated disclosure 65–73
Carlson, R. 14
change 114
climate 35–38, 142
Coleman, D. 137
communication
  apprehension 169–173
  attitude 2, 10–14
  competence 9, 31
  defined 41
  elements 27-29
  games 22–24
  incompetence 31
  model 27–29
  skills 10, 42
  styles 15–21
  time spent 7, 42
compromise 124
conflict 113, 114
  styles 123–125
  strategies 127–135
  structure 117, 118
cooperation and competition 120, 121, 124, 134
credibility 63, 163–165

delivery 169, 174–176
DiSalvo, V., Larsen, D, and Seiler, W. 44
discussion topics 82
dominance 1–2
Downs, C., Linkugel, W., Berg, D., 106, 110
Dover 44

Eadie, W. 14
Ehninger, D., Gronbeck, B., Monroe, A. 155, 156, 163, 166
employment interview 89–99
Endicott, F. 90, 101, 103
environment 30

equity theory 32, 75
expectations 5, 35, 54, 56, 57

feedback 34, 36, 52–54, 71–73
Festinger, L. 169
Filey, A. 133
flexibility 11–14, 58
Foster, E. 6

giving instructions 58
Goetzinger, C. 105
Goldhaber, G. 41
groupthink 138

halo effect 90
Hart, R. and Burks, D. 114, 123
Harvey, O. 20
healthy communication 24
Herzberg, F. 74
hostility 2

impression management 104–105
  first impressions 4, 104–105
influence 1, 2, 61–63
interpersonal communication 81–88
interviewee 100–103

Janis, I. 138

Kerr, S. 77
Killman, R. and Thomas, K. 123, 124
Koehler, J. and Huber 36
Kotter, J. 82

leadership 147–151
Leary, T. 2
Lerderer, W. and Jackson, D. 125
Likert, R. 73
listening 44–47
  problems 47–50
Livingston, J. 55, 56
Luft, J. and Ingham, H. 73

maintenance functions 149–151
management education 6, 7, 8, 41–43
managing and communication 6, 7, 41, 42
managerial success 6, 7, 41, 42
McBrearty, J. 100
McLuhan, M. 28
meetings
  attending 146
  conducting 140–145
  followup 145–146
  problems 137–139
  time spent 137

management presentations 153–156
  audience attitudes 157
  organizing 161–162
  room set up 179–180
  speaker attitudes 155
  steps in preparation 156–159, 166–167
  supporting materials 162–163
  using humor 168
McClelland 57, 58
McCrosky, J. 169, 173
Mehrabian, A. 3
Meyer, M. 107
Monroe's motivating sequence 166
motivation 41–43, 49–51, 73–79
  extrinsic/intrinsic 75
Muchinsky, P. 42
Myers, G. and Myers, M. 62, 67, 78, 79, 162

needs 34, 57
Nichols, R. 44, 50
nonverbal communication 3
Nunally, E., Miller, S. and Wackman, D. 16, 17, 18, 19, 20

Oliver, R. 157
Olson, S. 15
organizations and communication 29–36

Pashalia, Crissy 83
Pearce 61
perception 3, 4, 36
performance 78, 105–110
persuasion 3, 166, 185
Peters, T. and Waterman R. 7, 35, 41, 43
Phillips, G. 154
Piccolino, E. 165
power 65, 117, 125
problem solving and decision making 59, 138, 143–144
participative decision making 59
productivity 73
punishment 77

questions 84, 86, 91–97, 101–105
question and answer sessions 177–179

recognition 74–74
reinforcement 76–77
relationships 5, 6, 125
rewards 74–75, 77
rhetorical senstivity 11–14
risk taking 62, 64
roles 58–59, 115–116
Rosenthal, R. 54, 55
Rossiter, C. 61

Satir, V. 22, 23, 24, 25
satisfiers 74
self-fulfilling prophecy 54–57, 62
sensitivity 11–14
situational management 81
Skinner, B. 76, 77
Snyder, M. 105
Sprague, J. and Stewart, D. 168
Springbett, B. 90
Srivastva, S. 8
Stevens 44, 50
Steil, L., Barker, L. and Watson, K. 49
stress 68, 119, 120
submissiveness 1, 2
Swingle, P. 130

task functions 149–151
Theory of Reciprocity 1, 2
third-party intervention 134-135
Thornton, D. 103
threats 130
trust 35, 61–64, 73
Tschirgi, H. 89

values 5
Villardo, F. 165
visual aids 176–177
voice 176
vulnerability 61

Wallenchinsky, D. 173
Wilmot, J. and Wimot, W. 113, 117, 118, 120, 125–131, 135
Wyllie, J. 42

Zima, J. 97, 99, 106–108, 110

F